I0797155

## AN EMBROIDERY FIELD GUIDE
to the Textures, Colors, and Lines of the Natural World

ANNA HULTIN
Photography by Brooke Forwood

Storey Publishing

**The mission of Storey Publishing is to serve our customers by publishing practical information that encourages personal independence in harmony with the environment.**

EDITED BY Alethea Morrison and Gwen Hawkes
ART DIRECTION AND BOOK DESIGN BY Alethea Morrison
COVER DESIGN BY Carolyn Eckert
TEXT PRODUCTION BY Jennifer Jepson Smith

COVER PHOTOGRAPHY BY © **Anna L. Hultin**, front and back t.; © **Brooke Forwood**, back b.l., IFC, facing IFC, IBC; **Mars Vilaubi** © Storey Publishing, spine, back b., facing half title, facing 206, facing IBC
INTERIOR PHOTOGRAPHY BY © **Anna L. Hultin**, i, iii, iv, 5, 7, 12–14, 44, 46, 50, 52 l., 58, 64–66, 69, 71, 72, 85, 191, 192, 200, 206; © **Brooke Forwood**, vi, 3, 4, 8, 11 t., 15, 16, 18, 20, 26, 28, 30–32, 41, 60, 76, 114, 194; **Mars Vilaubi** © Storey Publishing, 9, 11 b., 21, 22, 24, 25, 27, 33, 35, 36, 38–40, 42, 43, 45, 47–49, 51, 52 r., 53, 54, 56, 57, 59, 61, 63, 67, 68, 70, 73–75, 77, 80, 83, 86–88, 90, 93–96, 98, 101, 104–106, 109, 111, 113, 115, 116, 118, 120, 122, 124, 126, 128, 130–132, 134–136, 138, 140, 142–145, 148, 149, 151, 152, 154, 157, 158, 160–162, 166, 168, 172, 174, 180, 182, 185–189
ADDITIONAL PHOTOGRAPHY BY © Flower_Garden /Shutterstock.com, 117 b.; © Lex Melony/Shutterstock.com, 117 t.; © Marcin Perkowski/Shutterstock.com, 117 m.

ILLUSTRATIONS AND DIAGRAMS BY © Anna L. Hultin



Storey books may be purchased in bulk for business, educational, or promotional use. Special editions or book excerpts can also be created to specification. For details, please contact your local bookseller or the Hachette Book Group Special Markets Department at special.markets@hbgusa.com.

**Storey Publishing**
210 MASS MoCA Way
North Adams, MA 01247
storey.com

Storey Publishing is an imprint of Workman Publishing, a division of Hachette Book Group, Inc., 1290 Avenue of the Americas, New York, NY 10104. The Storey Publishing name and logo are registered trademarks of Hachette Book Group, Inc.

ISBNs: 978-1-63586-845-6 (paper over board); 978-1-63586-846-3 (ebook)

Printed in China through Asia Pacific Offset on paper from responsible sources
10 9 8 7 6 5 4 3 2 1

APO

Library of Congress Cataloging-in-Publication Data on file

*This book is dedicated to my dad,*
*who would have been beaming with pride*
*if he could have held it in his hands.*

# CONTENTS

INTRODUCTION

# FINDING THE THREAD

On a bitter February night, I gave birth to my first baby boy in an operating room. He was breech, and I needed a C-section. I heard the doctor speaking to the nurse and the steady beeping of the monitor, until one slight noise caught my attention. I heard a breath. My baby's breath. He was here. I'd never met this person before, and yet I felt like I'd known him my whole life. All at once, what was strange became familiar, and what was familiar became strange—the first glimpse of how my life as an artist would become inextricably entwined with my life as a mother.

When we arrived home, I began to understand that the tectonic plates of my life had forever shifted in many ways, but the biggest surprise was how this new reality altered my creativity. Before my son's first triumphant breath in the hospital, I had created conceptual drawings and sculptural installations. I was interested in the confluent forces of the natural and the human-made—and the swirling weight of the extraordinary in the ordinary. My work had been occupied by the windows of a flooded, destroyed home hanging from a tree; the constant fire from an oil well's gas flare in a field where local cows pasture; fracking wells carving huge cracks through the earth's crust. Now the urgency of ecological disaster couldn't match the urgency of changing diapers and nursing the baby.

Still, I wanted to say something about the beauty and trauma of having major abdominal surgery to birth my baby, so I sat down to make a conceptual drawing about my C-section on a giant sheet of paper. I didn't have a studio, so I propped an old door on a pair of sawhorses and set to work in the laundry room tacked onto the back of our tiny house. The paper barely fit on the makeshift table. The laundry room was uninsulated and freezing cold. My efforts kept falling flat. I didn't have the mental energy to continue, so I stashed the drawing away. I reluctantly decided to set aside my studio work for the time being and surrender my idea of what being an artist looked like.

But I found that my hands still needed to *make* something. I kept thinking about how nice it would be to pick up a craft. Something untied to the art world. Something I didn't have to think too hard about. Something that my mother's mother might have done. Enter embroidery. Embroidery fit well into my new life as a mother. I didn't need a studio and could stitch on my couch, stowing my projects away easily and quickly. I also found great comfort in creating something beautiful just for the sake of creating something beautiful. My embroidery didn't *need* to comment on the state of our world. It just needed to be.

In this new season of my life, moments of the everyday and the ordinary had become almost painfully beautiful to me. Embroidery was a practical way to contemplate those ordinary things. Spending hours stitching the shift of colors and textures in the petals of a California poppy or studying the subtle brown of a patch of dead blue grama grass became small, intentional reflections on beauty that were just as meaningful and connected to the bigger questions of ecology and humanity that had always held my interest. In the years since, I've had two more babies and much has changed, but I never stopped embroidering. Stitching these subjects is a grounding, meditative process for me, and the practice has integrated into the rhythm of my life and my children's lives.

In both form and function, thread is the perfect material for exploring landscape art and nurturing a connection to nature. Thread can be line. It can be texture. It can stay in a hoop or spill out of it. You can layer stitch after stitch, which is perfect for building up layers of grasses. Conceptually speaking, thread connects: connects fabric and connects us to our ancestors who were embroidering centuries before us. What better medium could there be to link us to the land?

In the years before motherhood, I had always searched for a mix of abstraction and realism in my work. One day as my boys were napping, I sat down to stitch as usual. While laying down the stitches of a field, I experimented

with abstraction in an unusual way that finally clicked. All my embroidered botanical studies taught me how to create a field that looked realistic, while all the years I'd studied and practiced conceptual art before I had children helped me weave in the abstract. What had started as "just a craft" became my art form. Little did I know that through the simple rhythm of embroidering every day at nap time I would become the artist I thought I'd left behind—the artist I'd always hoped to be all those years ago.

## HOW TO USE THIS BOOK

This isn't your typical embroidery book. Although it has plenty of embroidery patterns for you to follow, more than anything this book offers in-depth practice of the artistic process—from the spark of inspiration to a final piece and everything in between. I hope you will learn as much about observing the land as you do about embroidery.

Whether you are picking up a needle and thread for the first time or have experience as a fiber artist, and wherever you are in the seasons of your life, my aim is to inspire you to grow in your creative practice. The projects are meant to build your skills and offer opportunities for discovery as you develop your own style and point of view. I'm excited to see how you'll take what you learn in these pages and apply it to your own observations of the world around you.

**CHAPTER 1.** We begin by learning how to look at the land.

**CHAPTER 2.** We review what supplies you'll need and how to set up a creative space that is both physical and mental.

**CHAPTER 3.** I share the fundamental skills of embroidering landscapes, from choosing colors and working with thread to my favorite stitches

and how to finish the hoop for a polished, wall-ready work of art.

**CHAPTER 4.** I share experimental methods for leveling up your landscapes, with unusual materials and techniques that I've developed over years of practice.

**CHAPTER 5.** I give detailed patterns and directions for four projects, which let you practice all the techniques and materials I use in landscape embroidery.

**CHAPTER 6.** I've developed a collection of over 40 designs for landscape elements—from trees, flowers, and grasses to fields and mountains. You can use these building blocks to stitch original compositions of your own.

**CHAPTER 7.** We see the building blocks in action, with patterns and directions for seven landscapes stitched from building-block elements. Stitch them as directed, customize, or browse for inspiration!

**CHAPTER 8.** I share tips for creating original compositions and wrap up key design considerations.

Before we dive in, I want to share that I am not a perfectionist. When I started, I learned only four stitches and didn't care to learn more until a commissioned piece made it necessary. I eat chocolate while I'm stitching and often get it on my fabric; my studio is messy and disorganized. If you look closely at any of my pieces, you will find inconsistencies in my stitching and maybe even coffee stains. My husband often says he is the only reason my work ever sees the light of day—as he moves hoops off precarious perches, out of reach of sticky toddler hands.

None of this bothers me a bit. I identify freedom from convention and perfection with the freedom to be experimental and unique and to adapt what has come before to fit my personal vision. I invite you to learn as much or as little as you need in the service of your own vision and to adapt my techniques to whatever feels right for you. There is no pressure here. Just a whole lot of fun.

CHAPTER 1

# CONNECTING TO THE LAND

Land is bigger than the human experience. In its self-reliance, the land exists with me or without me. Amid all the changes and challenges of my personal life, the land is steady and resilient, always available to offer comfort. Observing the land deeply and slowly is a practice in curiosity, humility, perspective, and reverence. Let's get started.

# CONSIDERING THE LAND

*Until we understand what the land is,*
*we are at odds with everything we touch.*
—Wendell Berry

Winter, spring, summer, fall. These are the fundamental ways that we begin to understand the land. The seasons helped us as children connect to the idea of change, time, and growth. As the seasons change through the years, we learn that all things come and go and come and go again. This cycle echoes our personal lives. In challenging times, I know that change will come, and I hold on to hope. Days of abundance don't last forever, either, so I savor the beauty of those fleeting moments.

The land has other lessons, too. The land accepts—accepts fires, floods, humans, and other upsets to its equilibrium. Through that acceptance, the land gains the power of transformation. Last year a fire decimated over half of the mountain forest near my home. When I looked at the devastation, ashes and stumps of burnt trees seemed to be all that was left. What I couldn't see yet was a new beginning. The lodgepole pines that once covered the forest have cones that release their seeds only in response to the high temperature of a forest fire. The forest accepted the destruction and created new life from it. Humans are not this way. When danger or hardship comes, we instinctively flee it or fight it. Because the land can't flee or fight, it stays and transforms.

## An Ode to Dead Grass

In the sea of grasses in a midwinter's field lies a single blade of dead grass. It had a life before its death. That life is spelled out in every crevice and line of its forlorn shape. It is a story—a little landscape all unto itself. There is a stillness to it: a peace and an acceptance. If we could cut out all signs of death from our lives, wouldn't we? A forever summer—but what is summer without winter? There is no life without death. If you recognize even a little beauty in dead things, that awareness can transform the way you see the world. Suddenly every part of the landscape is important. The mundane, the plain, the dead, the unsightly are all parts of a beautiful whole, sharing a communion with something greater than themselves. Suddenly there is a readiness to meet every moment of this life with expectant joy.

> Next time you pass by a patch of dried grass, pause. Look closer. Find some beauty there.

Perhaps delicate seed heads dancing in the breeze will catch your eye. The pale color of the dead grass might reveal a contrast of shadows in the field. Such moments of subtle beauty are worth capturing in needle and thread.

Dead grass is always worth stitching. A simple embroidered reflection on this patch of dead grass taught me about line and structure and made me appreciate the delicacy of the seed heads.

## How to Notice Nature

Building the skill of noticing takes consistent practice over time.

- Sit on the land. If land is scarce, gazing at even a single flower or blade of grass will do.
- Be open to wonder.
- Be patient.
- Find stillness.
- Find movement.
- Look for death.
- Look for life.
- Discover yourself as part of the whole.

## When Nature Feels Far Away

What if you don't live in a place that is surrounded by fields and mountains or any kind of natural beauty at all? When I talk about connecting to the land, I'm thinking about connecting to place. The place you live might be a city, or it might be a farm. If you can find beauty in your place, you cultivate a connection to it. This beauty happens everywhere, and you don't need to live near a vast landscape to find it.

I have found beauty in the way the light moves across my tiny kitchen throughout the day. Beauty comes to us unceremoniously and in the smallest, most ordinary moments. *Noticing* is what is important. Noticing is an exercise that helps attune our eyes to what is true and what is beautiful. If you don't have a real field to stand in but you've practiced tuning yourself to ordinary beauty, then you will be able to glean just as much inspiration from a photograph of a field as you would an actual field.

# SEEING THE LAND

Near a lake that I drive by every week is a small willow that bends toward the earth. The branches arc all the way down to the ground. In winter I see its shape as narrow fingers reaching toward the earth. Thinking of the animals that must seek shelter there, I imagine being small enough to hide inside, its branches like arms wrapping around me and creating a place to rest. Growing just next to the willow is a cottonwood that towers like a lumbering giant, arms reaching to the sky, or maybe reaching to find a friend. Cottonwoods never grow straight in Colorado. The harsh winds twist and stretch them so that they end up looking like acrobats dancing in the sky.

> If you want the land to come alive in your art, first let it come alive in your mind.

Look for a story written in the trees, the grasses, the rocks, and the flowers. Are the black seed heads that dot the winter fields just seed heads, or are they little birds that will come alive and float up to the sky? Find imagination. Find wonder. With patient practice, you won't be able to stop looking at the land in awe.

## Find the Quiet and Ordinary

When observing nature, we see the rush of a bird or the bright yellow of a wildflower first, but all parts of the land are significant, no matter how slight or hidden. Tune in to everyday beauty. When you are open to wonder and using your imagination, even the most ordinary and quiet things become important. Try finding what you overlooked. Does that humble fallen leaf have a beautiful topography of veins? Are the husks of seed heads on dead grass really dead, or do they hold all of next year's summer in their shells? Discoveries of what we've overlooked are often the most powerful subjects to make art about.

Another subtlety is juxtaposition. When opposites are paired, their individual characteristics are much more apparent than if they were on their own. This happens in nature all the time! The smoothness of the rock seems smoother when there is a rough patch of grass right next to it. Without the roughness, you might not have noticed the smoothness. If you want to highlight flowers dotting the landscape, you need to leave portions of your landscape free of flowers for contrast.

## Map the Movement

When I observe a piece of land, I see activity within the landscape, but I'm also looking for another type of motion—the movement of my gaze. While in your scene, close your eyes. Open them. What is the first thing that catches your eye? What is the second thing? The third? Ask yourself what moved your eye around the landscape. Was it a plant, a texture, or something else?

This exercise trains your eye to find compositional elements in the landscape. When you create a landscape with fabric and thread, you are doing the same thing. You are using the setting as a backdrop and adding elements to help your viewer's eye travel around the composition.

The next time you look at a great work of art, try this same exercise. Close your eyes. Then open them and notice the first thing you see. Then the second. Then the third. You'll become aware of how great painters masterfully lead your eye around the canvas. Our hoop is our canvas.

The movement of your gaze around a landscape reveals potential elements for anchoring an embroidered composition.

Sketching out the basic elements of a landscape can help you translate it into embroidery.

## Create a Mental Picture

I often teach students in my workshops how to envision a landscape for embroidery by laying a piece of tracing paper over a photo and tracing compositional elements. The sketch above highlights the key compositional elements I notice in a landscape; creating a similar drawing will help you do the same. In my actual process, I don't sit down in my studio with a piece of tracing paper and a photo. However, I do create a *mental* overlay of lines and textures when I'm observing a landscape in real life.

## Remember the Seasons

In summer, beauty is easy to find. We work harder to spot beauty in winter, but connections that are more difficult to win are often stronger than those that come easily. Our relationship with the land shifts with each season, affecting our perspective and our creative work. When you think intentionally and pause to take notice of these shifts, you can channel them even more clearly into your embroidery.

# SKETCHING THE LAND

Simple observation is the first and most important part of making landscape art, but a sketchbook will help you record your obser-vations. You might see something you want to sketch but don't have a sketchbook and drawing tool. I have drawn on a napkin or the back of a receipt using a pen from the bottom of my glove box. If I can't find paper or a writing utensil of any kind, I observe with patience before snapping a few pictures with my phone and then sketch when I get home. This process is incredibly flexible.

Begin by finding the landscape you want to sketch. Anything that catches your eye or strikes you as beautiful is the perfect subject, whether it is large or small, cultivated or wild. You are *not* sketching to plan a final embroidery project. The goal of this sketch is to soak in the world and let inspiration seep into your mind. Keep these sketches basic.

When sketching, I'm mostly interested in capturing the movement I see on the land that I'll later turn into a composition, and to do this I need very few details. I think of it as mapping out different elements in the landscape, always looking for what is moving my eye throughout that landscape. Here is how that process looks.

## Can I Sketch from a Photograph?

Not all of us live where nature is easy to find, so my answer is an emphatic *yes!* Will sketching from a photograph let you gather all the nuances and subtleties that you might have observed within the landscape? It might not, but you will still be able to glean enough inspiration from a photo to make a work of art.

Additionally, taking photos of a landscape that you are observing in person is helpful backup to the pencil sketches. Photos provide inspiration and guidance for selecting thread colors when you're ready to create a composition for embroidery.

## Build the First Sketch

Find a field, garden, or any natural scene (or look at a photograph of one).

Find a landscape that will serve as inspiration for your stiching.

**PLANT A HORIZON LINE ON THE PAGE.** A horizon line is the visual or physical boundary that separates the sky from the land.

**ADD SIMPLE DETAILS.** Roughly place a few elements and textures that make up the background of the landscape. This sometimes looks like patches of shading to show where the grass is especially dark, little circles to indicate rocks, or lines to suggest trees and hills on the horizon.

**DRAW SAMPLES OF WHAT YOU SEE IN MULTITUDE.** At this point you can add a bit more detail where there is an abundance of something like grasses or leaves. When I'm drawing a field of grass, I don't draw every blade of grass. Instead, I capture a few blades to document their size and direction. The same thing happens with a tree full of leaves. I don't have the time to sketch every leaf, so I draw the general outline of the tree and then fill in about a quarter of that shape with leaves.

**MAP MOVEMENT.** Once you have the backdrop of your landscape in place, start looking for compositional anchors. These elements are the most important parts of my sketches, but even still, they are incredibly simple. What parts of your landscape move your eye around it? Is it flowers? Trees? Rocks? Grass? Draw them as simply as you can, but be aware of where you're placing them in your sketch so that they guide your eye around the entirety of the composition.

Plant a horizon line and add simple details.

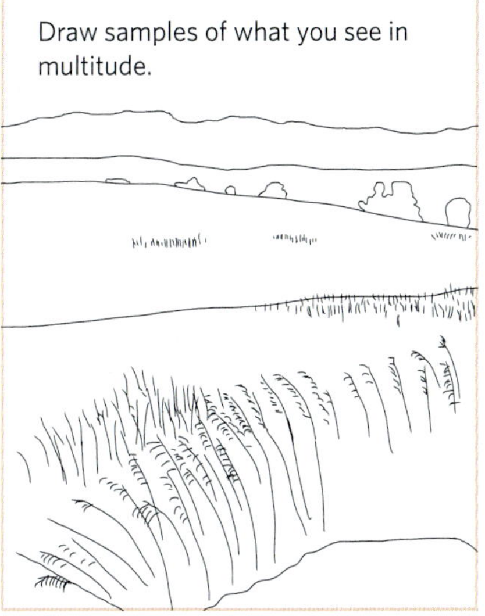
Draw samples of what you see in multitude.

Map movement.

## Next Steps

When creating landscape embroidery, first I soak up all the inspiration I can find from observing the land, sketching it, taking photos of it, and looking at other landscape artists' work. I call this my "sponge stage." In this stage I will also experiment with materials—maybe a new stitch or a new fabric that I want to try. I do all this without a specific embroidered composition in mind.

Next, I take all that inspiration and channel it into a specific embroidery piece—what I call my "studio stage." In this stage I'll create a sketch for an embroidered composition, choose thread colors and fabrics, and gather any photos that I need for reference. Then I'll dive into actual stitching.

But wait! Before you create your own completely original landscape embroidery (see Chapter 8), I recommend that you first read the chapters in between and practice with some of the patterns I provide. I've structured this book as a progressive workshop for building design and technical skills so that you are set up to succeed.

# GETTING READY

The only things you *really* need to start embroidering are a needle, thread, fabric, and an embroidery hoop. The best part? You can get all this for under $10 at just about any craft store. Another best part? The materials are small, lightweight, and portable, so you can embroider just about anywhere. Beyond the basics, I have tips about other useful tools and materials as well as on how to work with patient intention and find the time for creativity.

# GATHERING MATERIALS

Part of the beauty of embroidery is its simplicity and accessibility, and sometimes sticking to the basics will restrict your work in a way that forces innovation and creativity. A common pitfall is to spend a lot of time gathering supplies and getting everything *just right* before beginning when really you can simply dive in and add to your toolbox as you go.

## Sketchbook

You will use your sketchbook to observe the land as well as to sketch out specific compositions that you embroider. Any medium-size notebook—about 8" × 10"—will work well. You can also put so much more into your sketchbook: photos of art that inspires you, a flower you picked from a nearby field, pieces of thread, swatches of fabric, receipts, to-do lists, journal entries . . . anything! The best sketchbooks are ones that are *thick* and have all sorts of things glued into them.

## Needles

If you find yourself looking at the needle selection at a craft store and wondering which to buy and what the sizing indicates, you're not alone. After embroidering for almost a decade, I *still* get confused by needle types and sizing. Let me break it down for you. Embroidery needles are like basic sewing needles, but they have a longer eye for threading stranded floss. The larger the size number, the smaller the hole (that's where I tend to get confused!). I like to stitch with a size 3 or 4 embroidery needle when I'm using two strands of embroidery floss. For stitching with four or more strands, thicker threads, or yarns, I use a size 16 or a size 14 chenille needle. These needles have a much larger eye but still have a very sharp point like an embroidery needle.

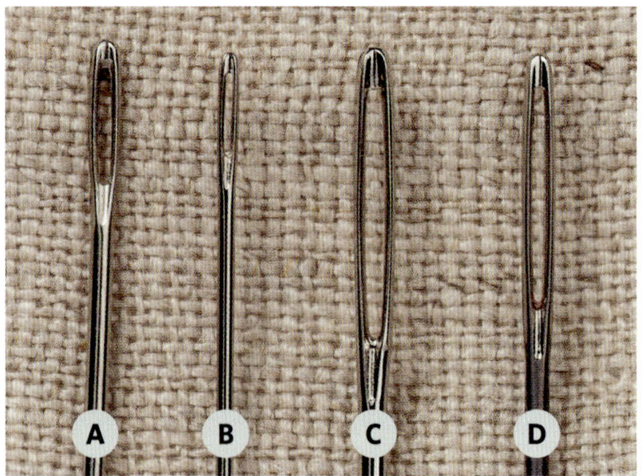


**A.** Embroidery, size 3; **B.** Embroidery, size 4; **C.** Chenille, size 14; **D.** Chenille, size 16

## Thread

There is no "right" embroidery thread. Yes, there are threads made specifically for embroidering, but don't limit yourself! If you can thread a needle with it, you can embroider with it. It may take some experimentation and determination to embroider with thick threads and yarns, but if you love the results, it will be well worth the effort.

**EMBROIDERY FLOSS** is the most common thread and what I use most. While there are other brands out there, I highly recommend DMC, found at nearly every craft store in almost every color imaginable. Classic embroidery floss comes in skeins. Every skein is made up of six strands of thread that you can separate or use together.

Besides floss, these are other options I love using, none of which are necessary but all of them can add interesting textures:

- **PEARL COTTON.** Created specifically for embroidery, pearl cotton is a twisted strand that cannot be separated into smaller threads. It usually has a sheen and comes in various thicknesses, sold in either skeins or balls. I find the balls easier to store without tangling.
- **TAPESTRY WOOL YARN.** One of my favorites, tapestry wool is a twisted yarn that can't be separated. It is typically the thickest thread I use.
- **TAPESTRY SOFT COTTON YARN.** Made for needlepoint, this yarn is five-ply and does not separate into strands. Its matte finish can be a nice variation from the sheen of embroidery floss.
- **HAND-DYED THREAD.** Sometimes I like to invest in naturally dyed threads, which can really enhance my stitching of grasses and fields.
- **WOOL ROVING.** Wool that has been processed but not yet spun into yarn, called roving, is technically a fiber, not a thread. I tend to prioritize selecting the color I want over the quality of the wool. I use it in such small amounts that any quality will work, but the color can make or break a landscape piece. To match the colors of the projects in this book, I recommend buying the Falling Leaves assortment from the brand Wistyria.

## Fabric

You can embroider on just about *any* fabric. Some fabrics will be easier to work with than others, but don't limit your creativity. When choosing a fabric consider the tightness and evenness of the weave. Higher-thread-count fabrics have a tighter weave; a lower thread count means a looser weave. If the weave is too tight, stitching can be a challenge. If the weave is too loose, your thread will pull holes in the fabric. I aim for somewhere in the middle.

Look for an even weave, which means that the lines of the weave are evenly spaced in a grid pattern and the fibers of the weave are all the same width. Cotton quilting fabrics have a nice weight and are the perfect weave for most of my projects. Kona Cotton is my preferred quilting solid. It comes in a huge variety of colors, but I usually stick with natural. I use linen or canvas to add texture and tulle to create transparent layers. When you're getting started, try raiding the remnant bins at your local fabric store so you can try out several different fabrics at a low price to find what you like best.

Whatever fabric you use, avoid prewashing it. Once your project is complete, you'll rinse it under hot water to shrink the fabric and smooth any wrinkles. Skipping the prewash helps ensure the fabric will shrink and be wrinkle-free.

*Note:* All the collaged fabric for the projects in this book use a blue cotton solid. Finding the right shade is tricky, so I recommend going to your local fabric store and looking at their various shades of blue. Waverly Inspirations offers a cotton in the color "glacier" that will be a close match to what is used in this book.

### Stitching on Tulle

Tulle is one of the most exciting and challenging fabrics to stitch on. I recommend using two layers of fine mesh tulle to give extra stability. If you want additional stability, you can place a piece of water-soluble stabilizer between the two layers of tulle. You will need to consider the fact that the backside of your stitching will be visible. Because of this I tend to use stitches that cover a lot of area (satin stitch, long-and-short stitch) instead of stitches that create lines (back stitch, straight stitch).

BASIC SUPPLIES
Scissors
Embroidery
snips
Sketchbook
Embroidery floss
Hoop
Needles
Fabric
Marking
tools
LEONIS

## Hoops

I like to have a variety of sizes on hand. When you are starting out, a 5" or 6" hoop will be the easiest to handle for practicing basic stitches. I like 10" or 12" hoops for landscape pieces. When choosing a hoop, look for minimal space between the outer and inner hoop. If there is a gap, your fabric will not hold, and you'll end up with snags and wrinkles in your work. I use every type of hoop: wood, faux wood, bamboo, plastic, and large quilting hoops. Bamboo hoops tend to be the best quality for stitching, but you can make any hoop work if the inner and outer rings aren't loose. I recommend rummaging through your local thrift stores, since older hoops tend to be better made.

## Marking Tools

While there are numerous methods to transfer your sketch to fabric, my favorite is the water-soluble fabric marker. You draw directly onto the fabric and then run the whole hoop under hot water when you're done.

Sometimes I paint with watercolor before I've transferred my pattern to the fabric. In this case you obviously want to avoid getting the fabric wet and removing the markings, so a heat-erasable pen is handy. You trace your pattern onto the fabric, and the ink will disappear when you apply heat from a hair dryer. Heat-erasable pen markings sometimes leave a permanent indent and slight residue on the fabric, so I recommend using them only when water-soluble fabric markers are not an option.

## Scissors

Fabric scissors are expensive and aren't necessary for embroidery work. A sharp pair of regular household scissors will cut fabric just fine. Embroidery snips for cutting or trimming your thread are worth the investment, though.

Because they are so sharp, they make clean, quick cuts, and their small size allows for more control, especially when cutting close to the fabric. I didn't use specialty embroidery scissors for the first few years I embroidered, so I would consider them nice but not necessary to have.

## Other Supplies

**BACKING FELT.** I like to stitch felt to the backs of my hoops, which adds stability to the fabric and keeps it taut for years to come, but this step isn't required. Look for a felt sheet that is big enough to fit your hoop. If you're backing a hoop 12" or larger, invest in a felt roll that gives you the bigger dimension you need. I recommend using a light color so that if you're embroidering on white fabric, you won't see the felt through the back of your art.

**BOBBINS.** I've seen people store their threads in all sorts of ways—even wrapped around clothespins or small sticks—but the most practical for me has been to wind my thread around small plastic bobbins. Sold next to the embroidery floss at most craft stores, these bobbins help me keep my thread organized and stop it from tangling. I recommend labeling each bobbin with the thread color number so that it's easy to match if you need to buy more.

Bobbins are a helpful way to keep thread organized and tangle-free.

**BOBBIN RING.** Keeping your collection of floss in a basket or box is great, but when I'm working on a project where I've carefully selected a color palette, it's nice to have a bobbin ring to keep those threads separated from the rest. The ring also makes transporting threads easy if you're stitching on the go.

**WATERCOLORS.** In my art practice, I often enhance my fabrics with inexpensive watercolor paint. All the projects with watercolor in this book use Marie's watercolor paint (from a set of 24 colors). Any medium-size paintbrush works well.

**DOUBLE-SIDED TAPE.** This is handy for collaging other pieces of fabric onto your base fabric. I secure the fabric with stitching as well, but the double-sided tape gives it extra stability. I like to use an archival-quality tape so that it doesn't harden or yellow over time.

# SETTING UP INTENTIONAL SPACE

The most important thing to know about setting up a physical space for your creative practice is that you can embroider just about anywhere. Keep your project in a small basket or bag so you can tote it around the house, or even bring it with you as you travel.

Different settings lend themselves to different types of work. If you are in the flow of filling an area with repetitive satin stitches or dotting the landscape with simple flowers, then you can easily stitch in front of the TV or with the din of a coffee shop around you. But when you are making design decisions about color and composition, a quiet space for mental focus will support your work better. That said, be patient with yourself and with your life. Do what you can, when you can, where you can. That will look different for every person. This journey belongs to nobody but yourself.

## Caring for Your Body

Keeping mobility in the body as you stitch is important if you will be embroidering for hours at a time. Make sure you stand up and stretch occasionally. I'm embarrassed to admit that one of my favorite places to stitch is in front of my TV, but looking up at the screen every now and then keeps my neck from getting sore.

To avoid eyestrain, stitch in bright light. Natural light is also an asset that helps with color accuracy since lightbulbs can significantly affect color temperature. If a bright, sunny spot isn't an option, you might want to invest in a crafting lamp. I like lamps from the brand Stella, which have a pure white setting.

If you struggle with carpal tunnel syndrome or arthritis, a hoop stand can help alleviate pressure on your non-working hand. Stands also are helpful for keeping fabric secure in large hoops. Since I don't use a stand, if I'm working on a large piece, I use a smaller 5" hoop and readjust the fabric when I need to move to a new section, transferring the whole thing to a large hoop once it's done.

## Finding the Time

Gathering supplies and finding the physical space to embroider are often the easiest parts of getting started. The harder part is finding the time and mental space. We don't live in a world that encourages slowness of mind and body, and embroidery is indeed a slow craft. I find that if I stay focused on *why* I embroider, *how* to make it happen follows, even if crevices of time between other commitments are all I have.

I am hopelessly addicted to productivity, which means that if I'm spending my time doing something, it needs to serve some purpose. When I sit down to embroider, my mind stills, my hands are busy, I am creating something beautiful. For me, this is all the purpose I need. I didn't start embroidering to make money or gain followers on social media. I started because I loved it. I found the time in my day because it was something I needed to do for my own mental health and joy. The desire to embroider motivates me to find regular time to commit to it.

## Creating Ritual

I've embroidered almost every day for over eight years, in part because I've worked the practice into my daily rhythm, stitching during my kids' nap time. One of the favorite questions that I've ever been asked is if I eat snacks while I embroider. The answer is *always*. The time I carve out of my hectic life for embroidery is precious, and I honor that by making myself a cup of coffee and treating myself to some chocolate. I often joke that the rest of my day is a countdown to nap time. Think intentionally about the time you spend on your creative practice, and it will become something you look forward to in your week.

Embroidery can become part of a creative daily ritual—complete with chocolate.

## Holding It Loosely

Make time for slowness of mind and body and see what comes. If I grasp for productivity, I feel miserable. I have learned to rest when I feel like resting. Some days that means sitting with my coffee and staring into space instead of stitching during the kids' nap time. Then I have days where I work with intense focus. There is an ebb and flow. When I hold the commitment loosely and let myself rest if that's what I need, I am so much more productive when I do have the energy. You've probably experienced something like this in your life and know you'll have to work to find your own balance. Nearly every artist I know wishes they had more time to spend on their art. We all do the best we can with the busyness and pressures of our lives.

### It's Not Just a Hobby

Making time for your own enjoyment can feel hard to justify. Embroidery might seem unimportant. It's just a craft, my inner critic says. As a mom, I've learned that leaning into the things that bring me joy provides positive lessons for my kids. I am showing them that:

- "Mama knows how to take care of herself. That is her job, not yours."
- "Mama has a life outside of being a parent. She's a person, too."

The balance between taking care of others and making time for art is a constant work in progress. I don't always get it right. If you are walking that line yourself, try to give yourself grace and remember that there is real importance to what you're doing for yourself.

CHAPTER 3

# ESSENTIAL TECHNIQUES

Have you fallen in love with a landscape and made a sketch? Do you have some basic supplies? Great! Let's plan the color palette, transfer your design to fabric, and learn (or review) the stitches. Once you've finished your embroidery, come back here for suggestions on how to prepare the hoop for presentation.

# CHOOSING YOUR COLORS

When you go to the store to buy your thread, or look through the stash of thread you already own, I recommend having a photo of the landscape or plant you are basing your piece on. It helps to hold thread up to the photo to find a good match. Embroidery floss is so inexpensive, I like to buy a lot of thread at a time, building in some flexibility to change or add colors to a piece as I stitch.

As you build your palette of threads, lay the colors out together. Often you'll find that a few threads don't look good with the others, and you can eliminate them from your selection. From there, consider the following design choices.

## Color Temperature

As I'm choosing colors for placement and composition, I usually categorize them as either warm or cool. Warm colors tend to come toward us when we're looking at an artwork, and cool colors generally recede; these tendencies are helpful when you're thinking about what parts of your landscape you want to stand out and what parts you want to remain in the background. I also think about color temperature when I'm considering the season I'm representing. Warm colors work well for summer and fall, whereas cooler colors work nicely for winter and spring.

Keep in mind that while yellow, red, and orange are warm colors, you can have cool versions of them. For example, add a hint of green to yellow, and the resulting yellow feels cool. The same principle applies to cool colors: You can have a very warm green even though green is technically a cool color.

I like every piece I create to include a variety of warm and cool colors. A landscape can be mostly cool with a few warm pops or have mainly warm tones with a variety of cooler tones thrown in. One thing I'll come back to over and over in explaining my artistic process is *variety*, and choosing colors is no exception!

## Contrast

Complementary colors lie opposite each other on the color wheel and create a lot of contrast and visual interest when placed side by side. If you have a green field and you want flowers

COOL

WARM

There are warm versions of cool colors and cool versions of warm colors.

Red becomes cooler when you add blue.

Green becomes warmer when you add yellow.

in the foreground to really stand out, the best color for those flowers would be red. If you want your orange California poppies to pop, try using a green with a lot of blue in it for the grass.

Complementary color pairs are red and green; orange and blue; and purple and yellow. These combinations bring a high level of contrast within a composition.

## Value

Value is the relative darkness or lightness of a color. When my grandma taught me how to paint, she always talked about the "darkest darks" and the "lightest lights," and those words have stuck with me. Your darkest dark is the absolute darkest shade of a color that you can find. DMC floss 935 is a great example of the darkest shade of green—so dark that it's almost black. A lightest light is just the opposite: the lightest shade of a certain color. DMC 3013 is one of the lightest light greens that company makes.

I like to classify colors as dark, midtone, or light, and I'll use those terms a lot as I discuss thread color choices. Often I'll be stitching a field of green with mostly midtones and lights and it will look decent, but once I add a section of my darkest dark green for contrast, it brings the piece to a whole new level. You want your landscapes to have a full range of values from the darkest darks to the lightest lights and everywhere in between. A piece like this will always grab more attention than one that uses only midtones.

Having a range of color values—from lightest lights to darkest darks—also creates contrast and interest in a composition.

## Brightness

I favor muted earth tones. My clothes, my home decor, even the color of my front door are all earth tones. When I started embroidering landscapes, I of course gravitated toward those muted colors. But one day I was trying to get some yellow flowers to stand out in a green field, and I just couldn't do it. I tried every shade of yellow I had in my stash.

As a last resort, I dug up a neon yellow that I received as a gift but never had any intention of using. Looking at it made my eyes hurt—that's how bright it was. When I added a bit to my yellow flowers, they suddenly popped just the way I'd wanted. Many surprises since then have taught me to keep an open mind with color, since often it's the unexpected choice that will make a piece sing.

### Color Palette Cheat Sheet

Decide on the overall feeling of the landscape.

- Do I want the scene to feel warm or cool?
- Do I want the scene to feel bright or muted?

After choosing basic colors, be sure you have a range of values and areas of contrast.

- Do I have at least several dark colors, midtones, and light colors?
- Do I have enough variety? (Are there bright colors added to an earthy palette or warm colors added to a cool palette?)

Decide what elements you want to pop in the composition.

- Do I want to grab attention with complementary colors?
- Do I want to spotlight elements with contrasts in temperature, value, or brightness?

Be flexible as you stitch, revisiting color selections. You may want to add colors or make substitutions as you go.

# PREPARING TO STITCH

Cut your fabric in either a circle or a square about 4" larger than your hoop. If embroidering on cotton quilting fabric as I do, I recommend using two layers, which offers extra durability as you push your needle in and out. When the fabric is a light color, the extra layer also hides any untidy threads on the back side of the piece.

Center your fabric over the inner hoop. Next, gently push the outer hoop over the fabric to secure it in place, positioning the hoop's tightening hardware at the top. The weave should always be straight within the hoop, not wavy or at a diagonal. You may need to pull the fabric at the edges to work it into alignment. Tighten the hoop hardware as much as possible, then pull the fabric so that it is taut and free of any wrinkles. As you stitch, you will occasionally have to retighten the hardware and fabric.

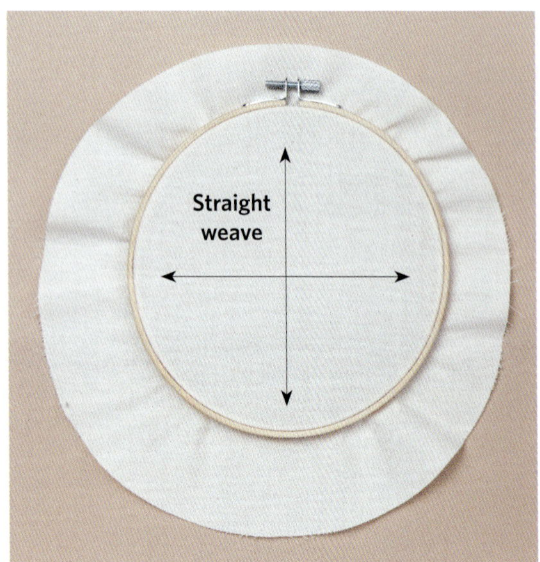


## Transferring Your Design

Water-soluble fabric marker is my favorite tool for transferring a design to cloth, followed by heat-erasable pen, but there are other options available. Many of the patterns in this book will need to be enlarged (and a few reduced in size). To do that, I recommend scanning the image and reprinting it at the recommended size. The following steps are suitable for either option.

**1.** Print or sketch your design onto a sheet of paper that is lightweight enough for light to shine through. The lines of your pattern should be thick and black, so if you sketched in pencil, trace over it with a marker.

**2.** Secure a single layer of fabric *wrong side up* in the hoop. You will be turning the hoop over and tracing on the right side of the fabric.

3. Tape your pattern onto a window or light box. Now hold your hoop up to the window so that the fabric is in direct contact with the glass. Be sure the weave of the fabric is straight, with the threads in horizontal and vertical lines, not diagonals.

4. Use a marking tool to trace your design onto the fabric.

5. Take your fabric out of the hoop and flip it *right side up*. Add a second layer of cloth underneath if needed for durability, and re-hoop. You're ready to begin!

## Other Transfer Methods

**WATER-SOLUBLE STABILIZER.** Using a stabilizer is often done in machine embroidery, but it works well for hand embroidery, too. A benefit of most water-soluble stabilizers is that you can print your pattern directly onto the stabilizer sheet, which helps if you have a very detailed design. When stabilizer is being used to support a delicate fabric, it's often applied to the wrong side of the project. However, if you're using it to transfer your design, simply print the pattern directly on the sheet and then apply it to the right side of your fabric. I recommend using a product with a sticky back for ease of attaching to your fabric. Once you're done stitching, take your fabric out of the hoop and soak it in water until the stabilizer disappears.

**TRANSFER PAPER.** Also known as carbon paper, transfer paper has a dusty pigment on one side that transfers to your fabric when you press on it. Sandwich the transfer paper between your design and the fabric, with the pattern on top, then secure the pattern in place by taping it to the carbon paper (or fabric if it overlaps the carbon paper). Using a ballpoint pen, trace the pattern, pressing firmly. I recommend using a colored ballpoint pen to easily keep track of where you have traced. The pigment from the transfer paper is rarely visible once you stitch over it but will wash out easily.

# WORKING WITH THREAD

One of the benefits of your typical six-ply embroidery floss is that you have multiple line weights to choose from when stitching your design. You can use all six strands together for a heavy weight or any increment down to a single strand for a fine weight. I use a size 3 or 4 embroidery needle when I stitch with one to three strands of floss. For any weights over three strands, I switch to a size 16 or 14 chenille needle, which has a much larger eye.

While thread is a forgiving medium, everyone deals with tangles from time to time. I have some tips to avoid that frustration.

- **PULLING FLOSS.** DMC winds their skeins in such a way that the thread releases easily in one direction. Find the end of the floss on the side of the skein with a color number and barcode on the wrapper. If you pull from this end, the floss will slide without resistance.

- **WINDING A BOBBIN.** Storing floss on bobbins keeps thread neatly organized and tangle-free (see page 28). I pull about 2' of floss from a skein at a time, winding the bobbin with each length until I complete the transfer.

- **SELECTING LENGTH.** Starting with an arm's length of thread will make stitching more comfortable and reduce tangling. Longer lengths of thread tangle more often.

- **SEPARATING STRANDS.** Separating strands of thread from a length of floss singly is prone to less tangling than stripping two or more at a time. Separate a single strand by holding on to it with one hand and catching the other five strands in the other. Simply pull on the single thread and it will slide free. You can join the single strands into two-, three-, or four-strand lengths.

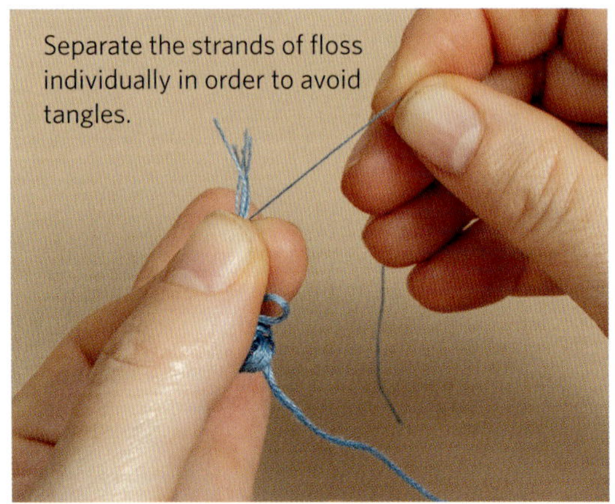

Separate the strands of floss individually in order to avoid tangles.

- **REMOVING KNOTS.** Knots still happen! If there were one tip I wish I'd known as a beginning stitcher, it would have been how to get knots out of my thread. Most accidental knots I see have a loop of thread on one side. Put your needle through this loop. Then pull the loop away from you while holding one of the other strands in your hand. The knot should come right out. If it doesn't, try holding the other strand in your hand while you pull away.

## Threading a Needle and Tying Off

To thread a needle, wet one end of the floss between your lips. Pinch the end between forefinger and thumb and then push it through the eye of the needle, pulling through about a third of your floss length. Tie a double knot on the other end, and you are ready to begin!

Once you're done stitching, bring the excess thread under a few of the stitches on the back of the hoop. Bring it through again, leaving a loop. Pull it through the loop to make a knot.

### Changing Colors

When embroidering a landscape, I don't necessarily finish with one color and then move to the next. Sometimes I switch between them and prefer to avoid cutting a new length of thread each time. When I want to switch to another color, I tie my thread off on the back of the fabric and then pull the thread through the excess fabric on the outside of the hoop, saving it for later use. I may not use that color again, but I like to have it on hand just in case. Plus, I love seeing the colors of my palette together once I'm done with my project!

# BASIC EMBROIDERY STITCHES

When I first began embroidering, I learned four basic stitches: backstitch, straight stitch, satin stitch, and French knot. A decade later these are still the stitches I use the most, with the addition of couching stitch and long-and-short stitch. If any of these stitches are unfamiliar to you, I recommend practicing them on scrap fabric before attempting a landscape. You don't need to master these stitches before you begin a project, but practicing them a few times will go a long way toward avoiding major knots and mistakes in your work.

## Backstitch

The backstitch creates a simple, straight line and is the best starting point for learning embroidery. You will get a feel for how tight to pull your stitches and how to find a rhythm. While I recommend practicing with stitches ¼" long, the length can vary greatly. If you are stitching a curve, use the smallest stitches possible. But for a straight line like a horizon, you might use backstitches that are up to 3" long.

**1.** Use a marking tool to draw a line. Push the needle up from the back of the fabric to the front at a point that is one stitch length ahead of the beginning of the line. Pull the thread all the way through.

**2.** Push the needle down through the fabric at the start of the line and pull the thread through.

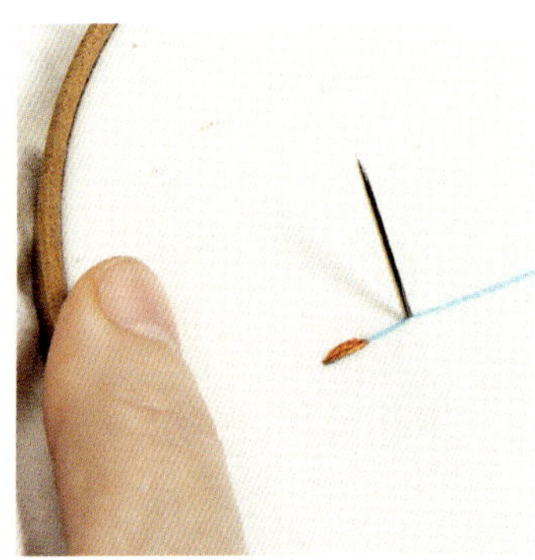

**3.** Push the needle up one stitch length ahead of the first stitch and pull through.

**4.** Push the needle down through the fabric at the end of the first stitch.

**5.** Repeat this rhythm of stitches until your line is filled in.

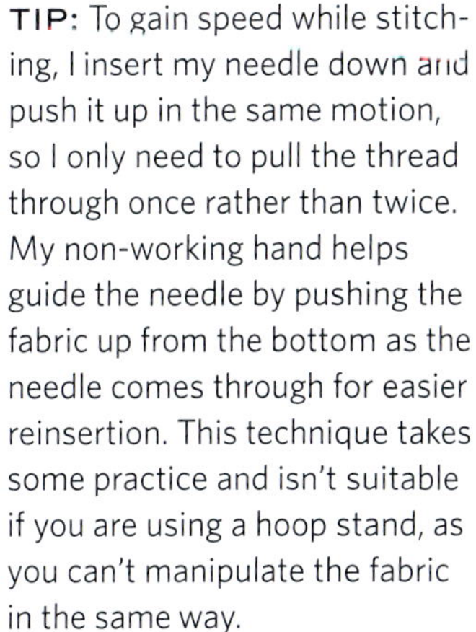

**TIP:** To gain speed while stitching, I insert my needle down and push it up in the same motion, so I only need to pull the thread through once rather than twice. My non-working hand helps guide the needle by pushing the fabric up from the bottom as the needle comes through for easier reinsertion. This technique takes some practice and isn't suitable if you are using a hoop stand, as you can't manipulate the fabric in the same way.

## Straight Stitch

Straight stitches are basically detached backstitches that can vary direction. These are essential for creating a large variety of plants and grasses in landscape embroidery. While I recommend practicing with stitches ½"–1" long, the length can vary. I don't typically make straight stitches longer than 2" (see Stitch Direction and Length, page 51). When straight stitches fill a shape rather than serve as freestanding lines, they are called seed stitches.

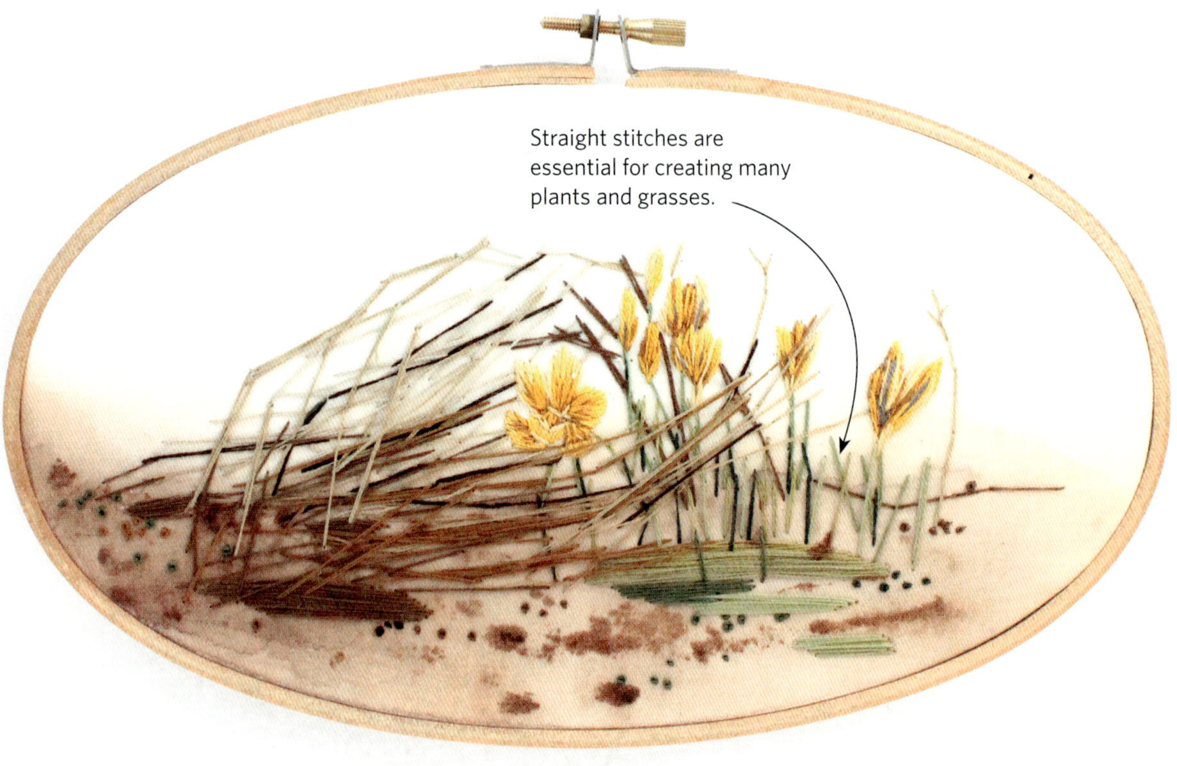

**1.** Use a marking tool to draw lines going in different directions. Push the needle up from the back of the fabric to the front at the beginning of one of the lines. Pull the thread all the way through.

**2.** Push the needle down through the fabric at the end of the line and pull the thread through.

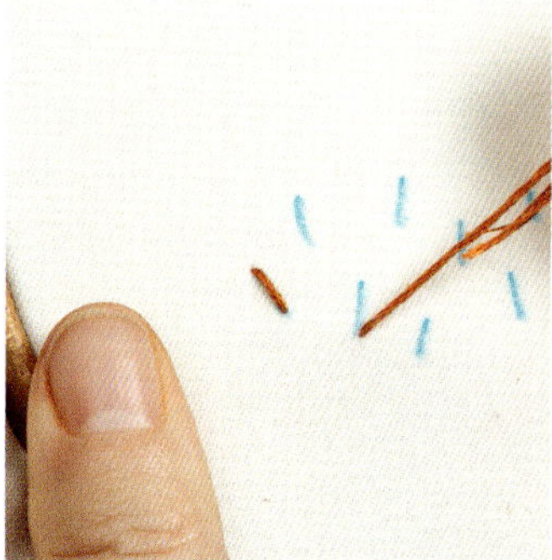

**3.** Push the needle up at the beginning of another nearby line.

**4.** Push the needle down at the end of that line. Repeat until all the lines are filled in.

**TIP:** When I'm working on a section of straight stitches, such as a field of grass, I work from one side to the other rather than skip around so that my stitches are efficient and I don't waste thread.

The back side of the hoop at right shows an efficient use of thread.

## Couched Straight Stitch

When I was developing my embroidery style, I started anchoring straight stitches at different points along a curve to make plants, grasses, and other forms look more natural. I later learned that method is called couching. With traditional couching, you work with two separate threads: a surface thread that you shape along the line, and a topstitching thread that anchors the surface thread at regularly spaced intervals. My method for landscapes is to work with a single thread that I anchor at irregular intervals—whatever is needed to achieve the effect I want. As always, I encourage you to experiment, too, and worry less about the "right way" to stitch. If it works for you, it isn't wrong!

I couch straight stitches for curved lines such as long bending grasses or the outlines of mountain ranges.

**1.** Use a marking tool to draw a curved line. Push the needle up from the back of the fabric to the front at the beginning of the line. Pull the thread all the way through.

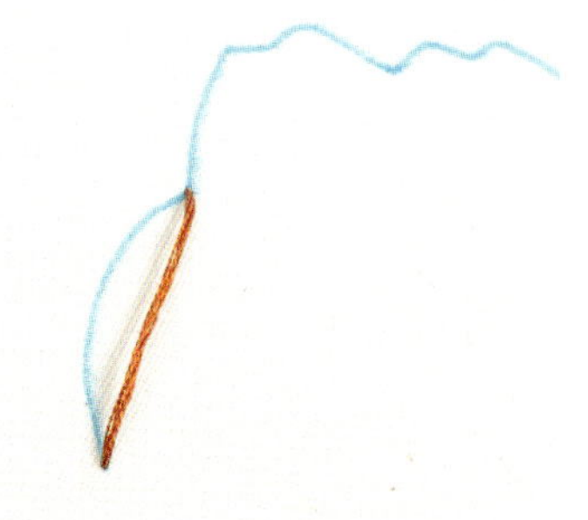

**2.** Push the needle down through the fabric 3" away or at the end of the marked line—whichever is closer. Pull the thread loosely through. We will call this our master stitch.

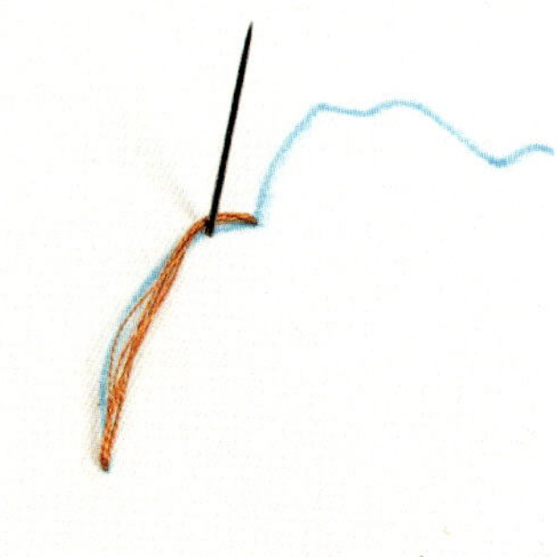

**3.** Find a point on the curve and push the needle up on the inside edge of the line. Pull the thread through.

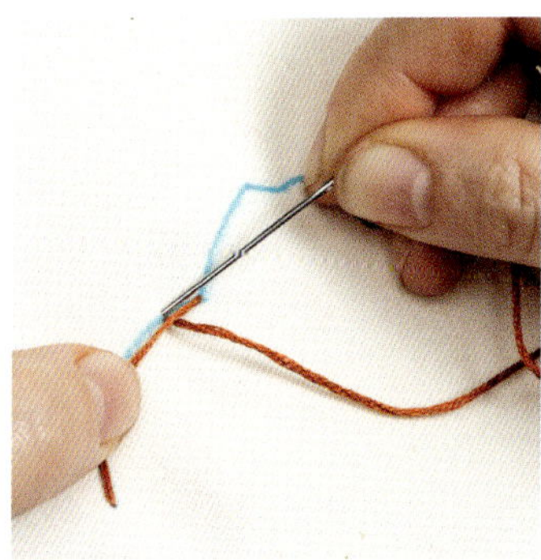

**4.** Push the needle down into the fabric on the outside edge of the line, next to the point where you brought the needle up, anchoring the master stitch along the curve.

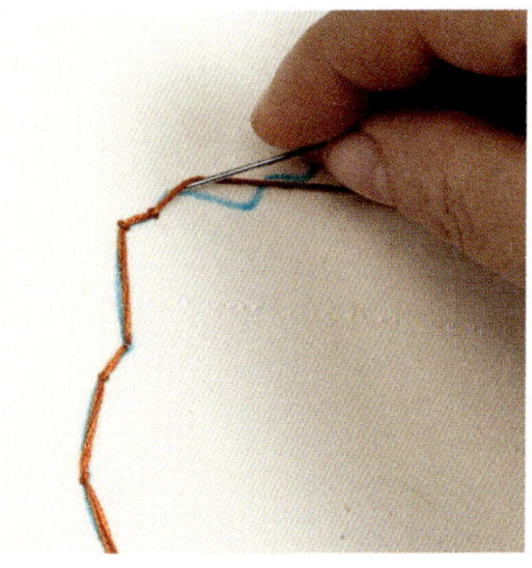

**5.** Continue to find points along the curve to anchor the master stitch until you have traced the marked line. If the curved line is longer than 3", you will need more than one couched straight stitch to complete the shape.

*Tips and troubleshooting on next page*

## Couched Straight Stitch Tips and Troubleshooting

**TEST THE LINE.** I use my needle to pull my master stitch to the marked line before adding a couching stitch to test that I'm anchoring at the best point for continuing the curve.

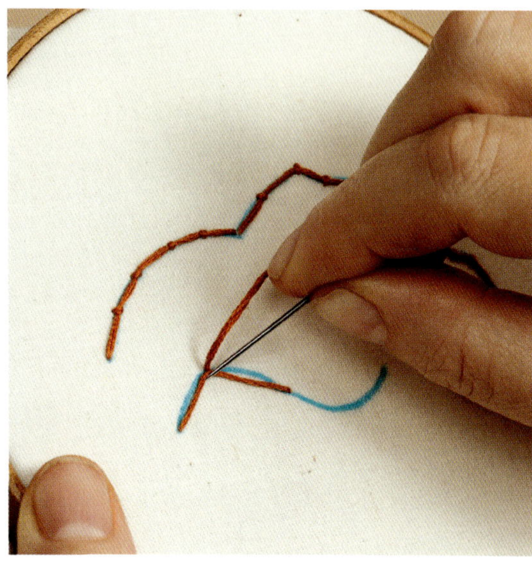

**ADD COUCHING POINTS FOR CURVES.** If your finished couched straight stitch looks like a series of straight lines with obtuse angles but you wanted a smoother curve, add more couching points.

### Lazy Couching Stitch

Instead of making small stitches along the length of the curve, sometimes I use another line to shape the master stitch. I often follow this method when I'm stitching a plant's stem. For example, create the stem of a flower using a straight stitch, which will be your master stitch. Make a leaf with another straight stitch, pushing the needle up at the tip of the leaf and catching the stem when you push the needle down at the base of the leaf. If you bend the line of the master stitch toward the leaf before anchoring, your stem now has a bit of a curve.

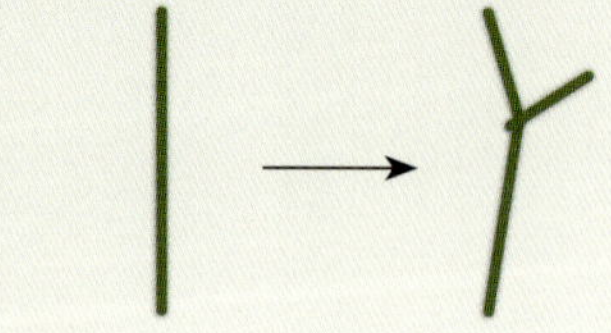

## Satin Stitch

Satin stitch fills shapes with a nice, even surface and is the stitch I use most, especially to cover a large area of the landscape. This stitch can be tricky to perfect, so be sure to read Tips and Troubleshooting on page 50 and refer to the sidebar Stitch Direction and Length on page 51.

**1.** Use a marking tool to draw a shape to fill in. Choose a side to start on and push the needle up from the back of the fabric to the front at the top of the shape. Pull the thread all the way through.

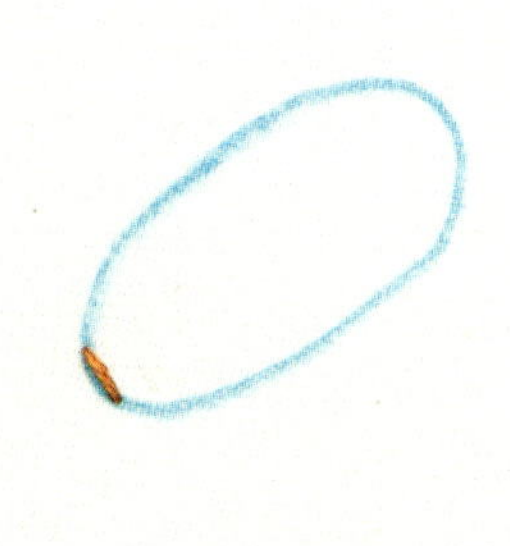

**2.** Push the needle down through the fabric at the bottom of the shape, creating a line as you pull the thread through.

**3.** Push the needle up directly next to the original starting point at the top of the shape.

**4.** Push the needle down at the bottom of the shape, directly next to the existing stitch.

**5.** Repeat to fill the shape.

*Tips and troubleshooting on next page*

Satin stitch fills large areas and shapes.

## Satin Stitch Tips and Troubleshooting

**THREAD WEIGHT.** Using four to six strands will help you fill in your shape quickly and create a smooth texture.

**UNEVEN EDGE.** For a smooth edge, find a consistent point on the outline of your shape to push the needle through for each stitch. I aim for the middle of the marked line each time.

even edge

uneven edge

**UNEVEN SURFACE.** The key to a good satin stitch is getting just the right distance between stitches. Too far apart and you will see fabric through the thread. Too close and you won't have a smooth, satinlike surface. Finding this distance takes practice, and it's something I still work on after years of embroidering. I err on the side of placing stitches too far apart, because I can always go back later and fill in the gaps.

**LOOSE THREADS.** When stitching with multiple strands of thread, I sometimes find that one strand stubbornly stays looser than all the others, but I have a quick fix. In order to realign all the strands so that they are even and to prevent loose threads, pull the needle all the way down the unstitched floss so that it touches the fabric, and then run your fingers down the unstitched length of floss so that the strands even out.

**LOOSE STITCHES.** If you notice loose stitches once you've filled in your shape, turn the hoop over, slide your needle under all the threads on the backside, and pull up to tighten the threads on the front.

## Stitch Direction and Length

Choices about stitch direction and length are important design decisions from both a technical and aesthetic perspective. The traditional rule for satin stitches is not to exceed ½" in length, but I have made ridiculously long satin stitches—up to 8"! The longer the stitch, however, the easier it will snag or come loose. If you embroider clothing, for example, the half-inch rule of thumb is advisable. That said, I keep my landscapes in their hoops, which maintains thread tension, and tend to hang them on the wall out of reach of little hands, so I routinely use satin stitches up to 2" in length.

Generally, you stitch across the shortest length of your shape to minimize the length of the stitches, but there are exceptions due to design considerations. When stitching something from nature, think about the direction of growth. With a flower petal, for example, I don't stitch across the shortest length because a petal doesn't grow in that direction. Instead, I opt for longer stitches going up the entire length of the petal to achieve a more realistic effect.

Use French knots for small-scale landscape elements.

## French Knot

Many people find French knots challenging, but don't worry! With a bit of practice, you will master them. I use French knots to create simple flowers and plants in my landscapes, and they are often the last touches I add to a piece.

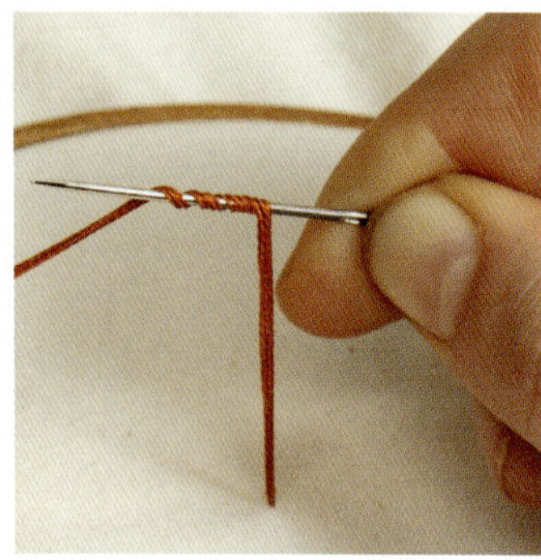

**1.** Push the needle up from the back of the fabric to the front at the point you want to add the French knot. Wrap the thread around the needle two or three times (even up to five!) to form a spiral. Be sure to hold the loose end of the thread securely with your non-working hand.

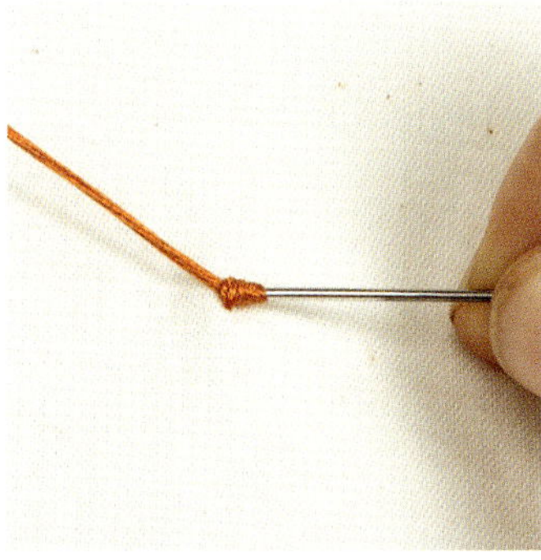

**2.** Push the needle down into the fabric directly next to the place you brought it up. Guide the spiral to the surface of the fabric, tightening the space between loops.

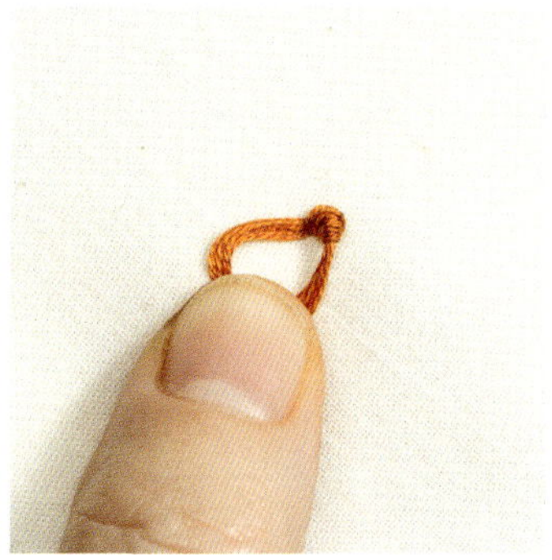

**3.** Keeping the thread taut, pull the entire length carefully through the fabric to create the knot.

**4.** Use the knot singly or in clusters.

## French Knot Tips and Troubleshooting

**DISAPPEARING KNOT.** If your knot is pulling through the fabric, make sure you're reinserting the needle *next to* the original starting point and not directly into the same hole. The needle must catch the weave of the fabric. Alternatively, your fabric weave may be too open for that knot size, in which case you need a bigger knot.

**TWISTED THREAD.** After making about 10 French knots, the floss gets twisted and hard to work. Use shorter thread lengths to avoid waste.

**TOO BIG OR TOO SMALL.** Increase the size of the knot either by using more strands of thread or by wrapping the thread around the needle extra times when making the spiral. Decrease the size by using fewer strands or decreasing the number of loops in the spiral. The minimum size is one strand wrapped twice around the needle.

## Long-and-Short Stitch

With the long-and-short stitch, you can overlap different colors in a gradient for an effect known as thread painting. The technique is like a satin stitch, but you vary the length of the stitches. I use this basic concept to create color variations in my landscapes. I recommend practicing with three embroidery floss colors that are dark, mid-tone, and light shades of the same color. For tips on stitch length, see Stitch Direction and Length on page 51.

**1.** Use a marking tool to draw a shape to fill in. Starting with the first color, fill in the top of the shape from one side to the other just as you would with a satin stitch, but use stitches of slightly varying lengths. The edge of the shape should look smooth, but the fill within the shape should be uneven.

**2.** Switch to the second thread color and fill the middle of the shape, stitching uneven lengths. Push the needle up at varying points within the first color so that you aren't creating a defined line. This variation is what helps create the gradient effect.

**3.** Finish filling your shape with one or more colors. The last color will still have uneven stitch lengths but should meet the bottom edge of your shape in a crisp line.

**TIP:** Use as many thread colors as you want to fill in your shape. The more similar the colors are and the greater the number you use, the more subtle and realistic your gradient will be. For more advanced techniques in creating a gradient with satin stitch, see Drawing with Thread on page 72.

## What's Wrong with This Picture?

When working with thread, there are common problems that most of us encounter regularly, so let's look at what to do.

### STITCHES ARE TOO TIGHT OR TOO LOOSE

Finding the right stitch tension takes practice. Too loose and the thread sags or pops away from the rest of the piece. Too tight and the fabric cinches, creating puckers. Err on the side of looseness, as that is easier to fix. See page 51 for tips on how to tighten loose stitches.

### FABRIC IS WRINKLED

Despite your best effort to keep the fabric neat, sometimes you get a stubborn wrinkle. Double-check that the hoop doesn't have a gap between the inner and outer rings. If there is a gap, find a new hoop. Also remember to keep tightening the fabric and the screw in the hoop through the course of the project. At the end of a project, you'll run the whole hoop under very hot water, washing out the water-soluble fabric marker and shrinking the fabric slightly, which eliminates wrinkles 90 percent of the time.

### THREAD IS HARD TO PULL THROUGH

Sometimes thread will be a bit too thick for your fabric and is hard to pull though. Try a needle with a larger eye, such as a chenille needle. If that doesn't work, you either need a fabric with a looser weave or you need to accept the challenge. Occasionally I'll use a heavier thread like yarn on cotton quilting fabric. If I were to use a thinner thread or a different fabric, the stitching wouldn't be so hard, but I'll suffer through because I'm looking for an effect that I can't get any other way.

# FINISHING YOUR EMBROIDERY

The only necessary step is removing residual pattern markings; I think the hoop itself is a beautiful frame for finished embroidery. If you choose to leave the piece inside the hoop, you need to cinch the excess fabric, and I also recommend backing the hoop with felt.

## Cinch the Fabric with Running Stitch

Cinching the excess fabric keeps it tucked behind the hoop for a neat finish. To start, cut the fabric on the outside of your hoop so that you have 1"–2" left around the circumference. I use a running stitch to cinch the fabric. Even though the running stitch is one of the most common embroidery stitches, I use it in my landscape art only for this purpose. If you find other uses for the stitch in your landscapes, that is fantastic!

To start, cut a piece of single-strand floss that is long enough to circle the perimeter of the hoop twice. Fold that length of floss in half and thread both cut ends through the needle without knotting it. There will be a loop at one end.

**1.** Anchor the thread by pushing the needle through the fabric and pulling it through the loop. Pull tight to secure.

**2.** Push the needle down to the left of the anchor and bring it up about ½" from there. Pull the thread through. Repeat this rhythm of stitches by pushing the needle down about ½" from where you just came up and bringing it up through the fabric ½" away.

**3.** Continue the running stitch along the entire perimeter, and pull to cinch the fabric.

**4.** Bring the needle up on one side of where you anchored the thread. Push it down on the other side of the anchor. Do this once more to secure the cinch. Tie the thread off in a knot and trim the excess.

## Removing the Markings

To remove water-soluble fabric marker, run the fabric under hot water. The bonus to this step is that cotton quilting fabric shrinks just enough to get out any wrinkles, giving the piece a crisp, clean look. I recommend using the hottest water available to get the most shrinkage. Make sure to keep the fabric in the hoop, which helps maintain tension during this shrinking process. Also be sure to get the fabric completely wet. If part of your fabric remains dry, you will get a water ring where the wet and dry areas meet. *Note:* If using a faux wood hoop, I recommend taking off the outer hoop for this step because sometimes pigment from the hoop bleeds onto the fabric after it gets wet.

The color of some naturally dyed threads can also bleed. If you are using naturally dyed threads, I recommend getting your hoop wet before you begin to get out any wrinkles, and marking your design with a heat-erasable pen instead of a water-soluble fabric marker. Then use a hair dryer on low heat to remove markings without damaging the fabric or any watercolor you may have added.

## Backing and Hanging Your Hoop

Cinching alone creates a tidy look, but I also back the hoop with felt for extra polish, which has the added benefit of securing the fabric's stretch. Take the outer hoop off your piece, lay it on a piece of felt to trace a circle, then cut the felt out and put the outer hoop back on. Decide if you want to use the hardware of the hoop to hang your finished piece. If you prefer clean edges like a painted canvas, leave the outer hoop off and create a hook from thread before attaching the felt (see Stitching a Hook on the opposite page).

Center the felt over the back of the hoop. Whipstitch the felt to the fabric around the entire perimeter. To start the stitch, cut a piece of single-strand floss. Fold that length of floss in half and thread both cut ends through the needle without knotting it. There will be a loop at one end.

**1.** Anchor the thread by pushing the needle through both fabric and felt. Pull the needle through the loop, tightening to secure.

**2.** With the thread coming out on the side of the fabric facing you, push the needle through both fabric and felt approximately ¼" away from the anchor. Pull the thread through.

**3.** Repeat this rhythm of stitches around the entire perimeter, spacing them evenly. Finish with a knot.

## Stitching a Hook

Use a pencil to mark a center point in the top third of your felt circle. Thread your needle with a 3' length of single-strand floss that is folded in half, leaving a loop at one end. Push the needle up about ½" to the left of the pencil mark and push it back down about ½" to the right of the mark. Insert the needle through the loop to anchor the thread. Pass the needle up and down three or four more times to thicken the line of thread and create a sturdy hook. Tie off the floss on one side of the felt and cut off the excess.

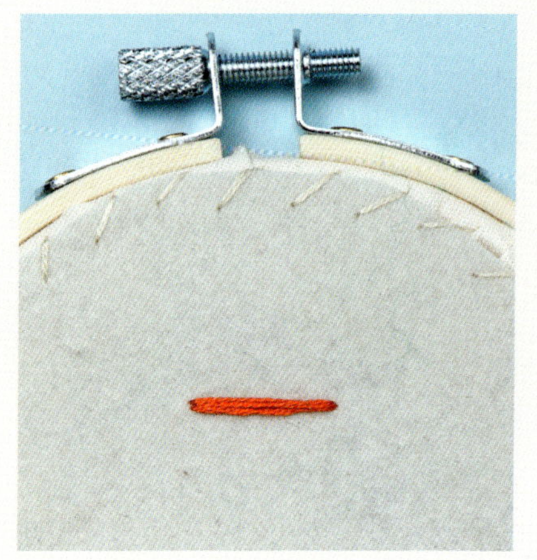

# EXPERIMENTAL TECHNIQUES

I have found many ways to work on fabric that aren't always rooted in traditional embroidery. Over years of experimentation, I've had many failures and a few big successes. Don't be afraid to try new techniques and materials yourself. The only rule is to create time and space for testing before you dive into a final work, so you remove the pressure of making it perfect. For every successful experiment, expect at least five failed attempts. Keep going! Art is just as much about the process—if not more so—than the product. In this chapter, I share some of my successes.

# WATERCOLOR PAINT

Watercolor on fabric is so much fun and adds an extra level of depth and interest to landscape embroidery. Ideally I lay down my watercolor first and stitch on top of it. Once there is paint on the fabric, though, it is harder to push a needle through. The thicker the paint, the more difficult it will be. If you are planning a piece with large sections of satin stitching or a lot of detail, I recommend adding the watercolor after you stitch.

Painting on a piece that is already stitched is obviously daunting, so practicing on scrap fabric is important. Since watercolor always looks much different once dry, let your practice piece dry completely before starting on your final piece. On evaluating the dried sample, you may want to add another coat of paint or change the color formula. Even after I've practiced, I sometimes keep scrap fabric next to me for testing each brushstroke before applying paint to the final piece.

Though you usually run the hoop and fabric under hot water as a finishing step (see Removing the Markings, page 58), you run the risk of washing away the paint if you've added watercolor. As a preventive measure, run the fabric under hot water *before* painting to remove wrinkles. Be sure to get the fabric completely wet to avoid a water ring where the wet and dry areas meet.

## Methods of Painting

I use a 24-tube set of Marie's Water Colour and a medium-size paintbrush. You have the choice of painting on either wet or dry fabric.

Wetting the fabric before painting will create the effect of a classic watercolor wash, and gradients of color are easy to achieve. The water in the fabric will dilute the color and the paint will "bleed," meaning that it will seep past the area that you got wet. If you want the watercolor to fade into the background gradually, this technique is the perfect choice. The caveat is that it's hard to predict exactly what is going to happen. Results will differ every time. There is beauty in the serendipity of that moment, but if you need more predictability, I suggest painting on dry cloth.

When you paint on dry fabric, you can more easily control where the paint goes, and you'll

## Mixing Color

Painters use a palette to mix colors, but you can use a paper plate or any nonabsorbent surface that you don't mind getting dirty.

I like my colors to mimic nature, and often the best way to achieve this is to mute the colors so that they are more of an earth tone instead of the bright color straight out of the tube. An easy way to mute paint is to add a bit of the complementary color to the main color. For example, to make red more muted, add a touch of green. Experiment with the proportions of the colors for the effect that you want.

When you mix colors, add just a touch of water. You want enough to loosen the paint but not so much that you water down the color. Once you have a color you might be happy with, test it on scrap fabric and adjust as needed.

get a defined edge. If you want crisp edges or more saturated color, then use this technique. The caveat is that you need much more paint to cover a surface area than with the wet method, because the color doesn't spread as easily.

## Painting on Wet Fabric

Start with dry fabric. Using a medium-size paintbrush, wet the area that you want to paint with clean water, soaking the fabric thoroughly. Now wet the paintbrush again, but this time pick up some paint and start adding it to your fabric.

Painting on wet fabric creates a soft transition.

The paint will flow freely wherever the fabric is wet (and will extend a bit beyond the wet spot).

Note that the area you originally moistened can easily develop a ring of darker color at the edge. If you don't like that effect, gently apply clean water to the edge with a paintbrush to discourage the color from condensing there. You can create a gradient if you apply a lot of paint to a localized area and let it bleed across the wet cloth.

Painting on dry fabric creates a defined edge.

## Painting on Dry Fabric

After mixing the color you want on a palette, add a bit of water, loosening the paint to a consistency that is easy to spread. Take care not to add too much water to the paint or you won't get a crisp, clean edge. Load the paintbrush with plenty of color and apply it directly to the fabric.

## Next Steps

Once you've achieved the color effect you want, let the fabric dry completely, transfer the pattern, and you're ready to stitch.

**LETTING IT DRY.** I recommend setting the hoop flat on a table to dry after painting. If the hoop is propped up, gravity can pull the watercolor down the fabric into places you didn't intend. Once it dries, evaluate the color. The paint usually looks much less saturated when dry. I often add a second or even third coat. Just repeat the same painting process as described earlier.

**TRANSFERRING THE PATTERN.** Since I want to avoid getting the piece wet after I've applied watercolor, I recommend using a heat-erasable pen rather than a water-soluble fabric marker. To be honest, I once got chocolate on a finished piece that had a watercolor background. I ran the whole thing under water to remove the stain. To my great surprise, the paint didn't budge a bit! I haven't tested watercolor's durability enough to ensure a consistent result, but if you're in a tricky spot, know that all is not necessarily lost.

**STITCHING ON TOP.** When you insert a needle through fabric that is thickly covered in watercolor, unpainted fibers of the cloth will push to the surface. If you remove stitches, those fibers become permanent spots, so take extra care while stitching. Also, the thread will pick up a little paint color with each stitch. Stitching with a shorter length of thread solves this problem because you will change the thread more often.

# WOOL ROVING

Before I started using wool roving, I'd spend hours laying down a field of satin stitches before stitching grass lines. Wool roving essentially created a shortcut. I can spend a few minutes laying down a background of wool and then stitch my grass lines on top of that. The added benefit of wool roving is that it brings an entirely new texture to your piece. The variation between the smoothness of the embroidery floss and the fuzziness of the wool makes the surface come alive.

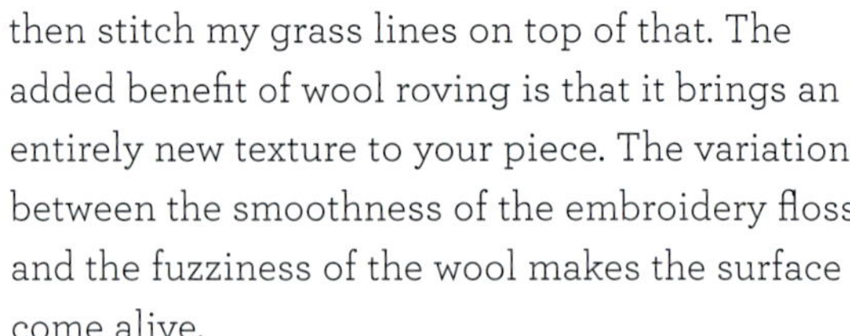

Wool roving covers large surface areas with rich texture.

## Laying Out the Wool

Spread the wool out in the area you want to use it and even a bit beyond the area's border, as roving tends to clump. Use the needle to gently comb the wool, guiding the fibers where you want them to lie. In general, using more wool is better than less, because it's easier to take wool away than add it. As you experiment, you'll get a feel for the right amount.

You'll notice that the wool stretches more in one direction than the other. By working in the direction of the easy pull, you can stretch the wool thin, creating a fading effect at the edges.

## Attaching the Wool

Using embroidery floss that is a close color match, anchor the wool to the fabric with a few small stitches directly on top of the wool. I find it helpful to put some of these stitches close to the edge of

Tack the wool to the fabric with anchor stitches if you intend to satin stitch over an edge.

After tacking the wool, I usually attach it permanently with a row of satin stitches.

An alternative option for attaching the wool is to stitch in the middle.

the wool because that is where the wool will catch and pull as you stitch other parts of the hoop.

From here you have a couple of options. Sometimes I attach the edge of the wool with a line of satin stitching. Avoid pushing the needle from the back of the fabric up through the roving because you'll catch pieces of wool in your fingers. I begin my satin stitch ½" away from the wool and push the needle down through the wool. Using the hand that is holding the hoop to also hold down the wool helps keep the roving from drifting.

If I don't want to satin stitch directly into the wool, I do a row of satin stitches by itself and lay my wool next to it. Then I lay down anchor stitches to attach the wool by going over my existing satin stitch but extending it through the wool.

Another option, which can be used on its own or in conjunction with satin stitching, is to stitch in the middle of the wool area. Because of the thickness of the roving, stitches don't always show up at first. You may need to pass over an area several times. Longer stitches tend to show up better than small ones, and the more you add, the more they will stand out as the wool becomes pinned down.

You can fully enclose a section of wool with satin stitching on all sides, or you can leave part of it free for a gentler color transition to the

Satin stitching at top and bottom creates a crisp edge.

Leaving the wool loose on three sides creates a gentle transition to the background fabric.

background fabric. When I am leaving part of the wool hanging, I lay it out vertically so that it can stretch and fade in the right direction. Try the experiments in the section Drawing with Thread (page 72) using roving. What stitches show up? Which ones are harder to see? Which colors work well together?

## Finishing the Wool

If you have more wool than you want, either pull out portions with your hands or cut off the excess with embroidery snips. Pulling it out will leave wispy strands; cutting it will give a clean line. If you cut the wool, tiny fibers will drop onto the background fabric and can make it look messy. Use a damp cloth to gently clean up the trimmings.

# FABRIC COLLAGE

Fabric can be collaged just like paper. Collaging just about any fabric on top of your base fabric brings new and exciting textures to your work. The method I use for attaching the fabrics is only suitable for pieces that hang on a wall. If your piece will experience wear and tear, I recommend buying a fusible web that bonds two pieces of fabric when heat is applied.

## Prepping the Fabric

Cut your fabric into any shape. I personally love the frayed edges of cut fabric and want that to show on my final piece. For clean edges, cut your fabric a little larger than the desired size so that you can fold and press the edges under with a hot iron.

Try out different compositions by laying your fabric on top of your base layer. Test different angles and dimensions. You might be surprised at what ends up working best!

## Attaching the Fabric

Attach double-sided tape to the back of your collage fabric at its edges. Position the collage fabric on the base fabric and press to stick the tape. Secure along the edge of the shape with a

small stitch every 2". If you are using a transparent fabric, like mesh, skip the double-sided tape and simply stitch.

Layering embroidery on top of the collaged fabric further secures the fabric. Take care with where you bring the needle up, because if it comes through the double-sided tape, it may get sticky. Try to avoid those areas or use a needle reserved for this purpose.

If you change your mind about where to position the collaged fabric and need to move it, you might find residual tape on the base fabric. Rub your finger quickly over the tape, and the oil from your skin should release it.

Once the tape is affixed, peel off the paper to reveal the second sticky side.

Embroidering over the collaged fabric integrates it into the design, but avoid stitching through the tape.

# THREAD DRIPS

I first created a drip effect in my embroidery during an attempt to blend the threads of the landscape with the weave of the base fabric. I don't know that I succeeded in my original goal, but I loved the abstraction of the drips in an otherwise realistic landscape. When choosing colors, I usually try to echo the same threads that are directly above the drips in the landscape.

## Marking and Stitching the Drips

There is no need to plan every drip line, but it's helpful to mark the border of the area that you want your drips to reach. Begin with a series of six-strand straight stitches that fill half the depth of the marked area. These stitches should be very close together—almost as tight as a satin stitch—and end at varying lengths, unlike a satin stitch.

Now switch to two-strand straight stitches that extend from the top of the drip area to the bottom. They should be a lot farther apart than the thicker stitches you just did. To get the drips perfectly vertical or to land in a certain spot, bring the needle up through the bottom of the marked area and then pull the thread through. With your free hand, lay the thread against the fabric and test where you want the drip line to reenter. Mentally note where this point is before pushing the needle through.

Occasionally I want drips with organic curves, almost like roots. To achieve this look, use a couched straight stitch or lazy couching stitch (see page 48).

Drips begin with a band of six-strand straight stitches.

Two-strand straight stitches extend from the top of drip area to the bottom.

# DRAWING WITH THREAD

Drawing is my first love. I love its immediacy—the way drawing shows the artist's hand, how the process of sketching one's thoughts is a record of time, and how the ease of adding a line to a page is equal to the ease of erasing it. I am often more interested in famous artists' sketchbooks than their finished works.

The basis of drawing is line, and I have always seen thread as line. Line can create composition, value, shape, tone, and texture. What you can create with a single thread is limitless when you see it as line.

While learning traditional embroidery techniques is helpful, it is equally important in landscapes to be free with your line work and let the thread guide your hand. Sometimes I'll just drop a piece of thread onto my stretched fabric to see how it falls naturally and then try to re-create that line with stitching.

Inspiration often comes from playfulness, so I encourage you to play with your materials and your technique. Here are some exercises to get you started.

You might use dozens of lines in tightly controlled, parallel satin stitches to create the smooth petal of a flower.

Or you might overlap hundreds of lines freely in all directions to create textured grass.

## Find Your Line

This exercise trains your mind to see thread as line and captures an organic curve with the help of gravity.

**1.** Hold a 6" length of thread above a piece of fabric. Let it fall. Use a water-soluble fabric marker to trace the line the thread made, then trace the line with a backstitch.

**2.** Repeat the same process using a couched straight stitch. Notice the difference in line quality compared to the backstitch. One isn't necessarily better than the other, but pay attention to the difference.

**3.** Repeat these processes on the same fabric four or five more times to create overlapping lines. Get creative! Use different colors, different threads, or multiple shades of one color.

### How Do I Erase Stitches?

While not as easy as erasing pencil on paper, removing stitches from fabric is quite flexible. If you want to make a change, you can use embroidery snips to cut the thread and pull your stitching out. Sometimes you can simply stitch over the part you don't like. I do this more often than I want to admit, but it adds depth and interest to the work when I do!

*Draw lines, young man,*
*and still more lines, both from life*
*and from memory, and*
*you will become a good artist.*

—Jean-Auguste-Dominique Ingres,
to Edgar Degas

## Create a Gradient

With paper and pencil, an artist can shade an area from light to dark as they move across the page. We are going to shade with thread.

**1.** Choose threads in at least three shades of the same color (light red, medium red, and dark red, for example). With a water-soluble fabric marker, draw a shape 1"-2" wide and any length. The shape might be an abstract blob, a flower petal, or something else.

**2.** Use four- to six-strand floss. Starting with the lightest shade of your color, use satin stitch to fill part of the shape. Follow with one or more midtones and then the darkest shade.

**3.** To blend the colors, use two-strand floss. Starting with the darkest shade, bring the needle up where the dark tone meets the midtone and add a few stitches on top of the midtone. If the shift from one shade to the other still feels too abrupt, you can go in the opposite direction, bringing midtone thread into the dark tone. Once the line between the shades has softened, repeat the same process of blending the midtone and light tone.

## Get Consistently Inconsistent

Making marks that vary in size, shape, and consistency is quite easy with a pencil. When you stitch with thread, you can vary stitch lengths, stitch types, thread types, and thread weights. Look for variation in all ways! The key to making embroidered landscapes look natural is variation, because nature itself is not homogeneous. If you stitch a field of flowers, for example, and every flower is spaced the same distance apart, the field won't look realistic. Similarly, a single flower won't look realistic if every petal is the same size and shape and facing the same direction. There is always a certain amount of asymmetry and nonuniformity in the natural world. For this exercise we'll stitch shapes that are spaced unevenly to create organic movement.

**1.** Using six-strand floss, make ten or fifteen satin stitches in the shape of an irregular oval. Satin stitch five additional ovals the same way, spacing them unevenly within the hoop.

2. Now create four smaller shapes, using two stitches for each shape. Place these shapes near the ovals but at different distances each time.

3. Distribute five or six small, single stitches around the other shapes.

4. Look over your composition. Are there any awkward gaps? Are there spots where you placed elements with unnatural consistency? Assess, adding or removing shapes and stitches as needed.

## Make Layers

My favorite pencil drawings are layered. You begin with a sketch in light pencil and then gradually build up layers of graphite to create different shades and textures. I do the same thing with stitches when I draw with thread. I start with one type of stitch, and I'm not afraid to layer different stitches on top!

1. Fill a shape with satin stitch.

2. Switch to a new color and layer some freestanding straight stitches in different directions on top. Work your needle between the existing satin stitches, taking care not to split the threads.

3. Switch colors again and make some French knots on top of the straight stitches. Try different sizes of French knots to create variation.

4. Fill in any gaps that opened in the bottom layer with additional satin stitches.

CHAPTER 5

# PRACTICE PROJECTS

Let's apply the techniques you've learned to four landscapes, stitched from photographs taken in the same spot in the same field at four different times of year. We'll begin in winter and add new abilities and complexities with each season, growing and developing skills alongside the growing plants in the field. From the experience you build with these projects, you'll have the confidence and capability to compose original embroidered landscapes.

# WHAT TO KNOW BEFORE YOU START

If you are reading this book in the middle of summer, I still want you to start with the winter field, because you'll practice the basic skills needed to move on to more complex pieces.

Each landscape has a color and stitch guide as well as a traceable pattern. Sometimes there is more than one pattern because there are multiple layers to the composition. I've separated them into layers to ensure the patterns are simple to read and use. The first pattern is for the middle ground and the second for the foreground. (Find more on middle ground and foreground on the facing page.)

I use a water-soluble fabric marker and the window method to transfer the middle-ground pattern onto the fabric (see page 38). Once you've stitched the middle ground, mark or stitch the foreground details freehand, using the second pattern for reference.

### Overcoming Challenges

I wasn't sure how I'd make four unique compositions based on one field, and there were challenges along the way. I wanted to capture bright yellow rabbitbrush in fall, for example—in fact, you could say the whole idea hinged on it—but an unseasonably early snowfall killed the rabbitbrush before I could photograph its autumn color. The lesson is that nature, and art, is always unpredictable, but I'll walk you through my design process for each project and demonstrate how to push through problems.

## Landscape Compositions

I see landscapes as vignettes of wonder, color, and movement. I intentionally leave negative space around my landscapes to create a portal of imagination for the viewer, clearing ambient clutter and creating a quiet moment of beauty in the chaos of our world. When you design original compositions, you can do the same or stitch to fill the entire hoop, depending on your vision and inclination.

Either way, landscape compositions have a middle ground, background, and foreground. I recommend you work on the sections in that order but keep a steady awareness of all three components as you sketch and stitch.

**THE MIDDLE GROUND** is the bulk of the landscape and the bulk of the stitching. Consider it the large backdrop onto which you'll stitch details. This layer is mostly satin stitched, sometimes with sections of wool roving. The top of your middle ground is the horizon line. Though technically the part of the middle ground nearest the horizon is background and the lowermost part is foreground, I identify the entirety of the satin-stitched base as middle ground for clarity in the patterns and stitch guides.

**THE BACKGROUND** of the piece is usually the sky and any details like trees or mountains that sit atop the horizon line.

**THE FOREGROUND** is the top layer of the composition. These are details such as flowers or small plants that pop out from the middle ground and carry the eye around the composition. In these practice landscapes, your foreground details will (and should!) look different than mine. I'll give you the general size and direction of the blades in a patch of grass, but you'll add however many you want. Follow your intuition, and you'll make the pattern your own.

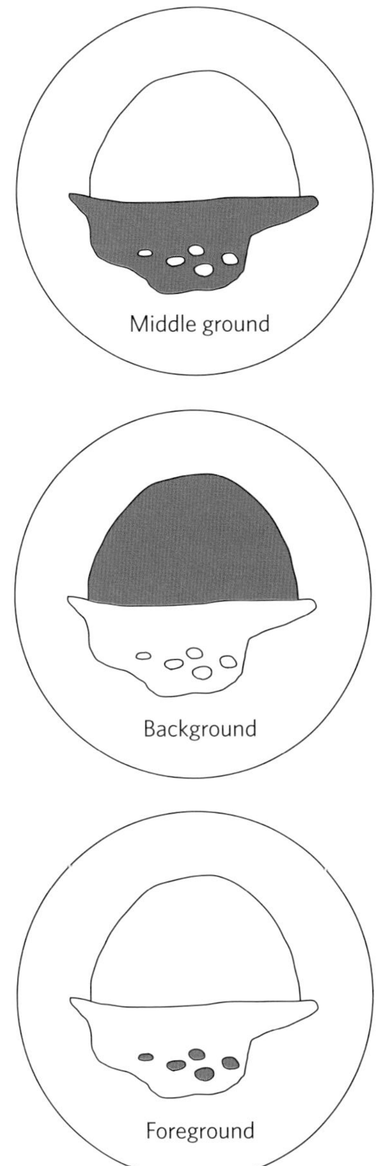

# WINTER

*I prefer winter and fall, when you can feel the bone structure in the landscape—the loneliness of it, the dead feeling of winter. Something waits beneath it, the whole story doesn't show.*

—Andrew Wyeth

Winter. Summer's bounty and energy have faded, leaving time for quiet contemplation and time for rest. Rest for humans under blankets in the warmth of our homes. Rest for the seeds asleep under snow. All of us are waiting with expectant hope for the promise of spring. The sky seems larger and bluer against the browns of the dead landscape. The plants and fields show their understructure: the fibers that make up their stems and seed heads.

The very first landscape I embroidered was a winter landscape. Winter is the perfect season to start with, since the bones of the landscape are obvious and building a composition is easier.

## MY DESIGN PROCESS

When I first looked at the photo on page 76 (upper left), the dead rabbitbrush in the foreground stood out to me the most. I decided to make those two plant clusters the central focus of the piece. I placed them in my foreground and gave them the most detail. From there I wanted to capture the patchy dead grass showing through the melted snow. I noticed that I could see a lot more texture and detail in the foreground, but the patches merged in the background. To achieve something similar in my hoop, I satin stitched patches of brown farther apart in my foreground. As the grass patches went back in space, they gradually merged into one continuous area of satin stitching at the horizon line.

The wispy grass between the two rabbitbrush clusters kept catching my eye. I was tempted to stitch them in detail because of how beautifully they struck me, but I decided that would detract attention from the rabbitbrush. I stitched these grasses as a few simple lines without putting too much emphasis on detail.

The white of the snow creates negative space in the embroidery, highlighting the patches of dried plants and grasses. These patches lead our eyes around the piece, from the rabbit-brush in the front, up to and across the horizon line, then back to the second rabbitbrush, with the long lines of the individual blades of dried grass guiding us back to the starting point.

The biggest struggle I faced with this landscape was determining the level of abstraction I wanted. I had planned on more negative space, but after stitching the horizon line, central patches of grass, and rabbitbrush, the composition looked too spare and unfinished. I took a photo of the embroidery and sketched out different ideas. I landed on adding patches of satin-stitched grass closer to the edge of the hoop for balance.

## COLOR AND STITCH GUIDE

| CODE LETTER | STITCHES |
|---|---|
| **A** | Satin stitch |
| **B** | Straight stitch |
| **C** | Couched straight stitch |
| **D** | French knot |

| CODE NUMBER | MARIE'S WATERCOLOR PAINTS |
|---|---|
| **9** | Cerulean blue + Lamp black |

| CODE NUMBER | DMC EMBROIDERY FLOSS COLOR # |
|---|---|
| **1** | 611 |
| **2** | 869 |
| **3** | 801 |
| **4** | 520 |
| **5** | 782 |
| **6** | 422 |
| **7** | 613 |
| **8** | 612 |
| **9** | 433 |

### OTHER MATERIALS

- Basic supplies (see Chapter 2), including a 10" embroidery hoop and two layers of Kona cotton quilting fabric (in natural), cut into a 14" circle
- Paintbrush

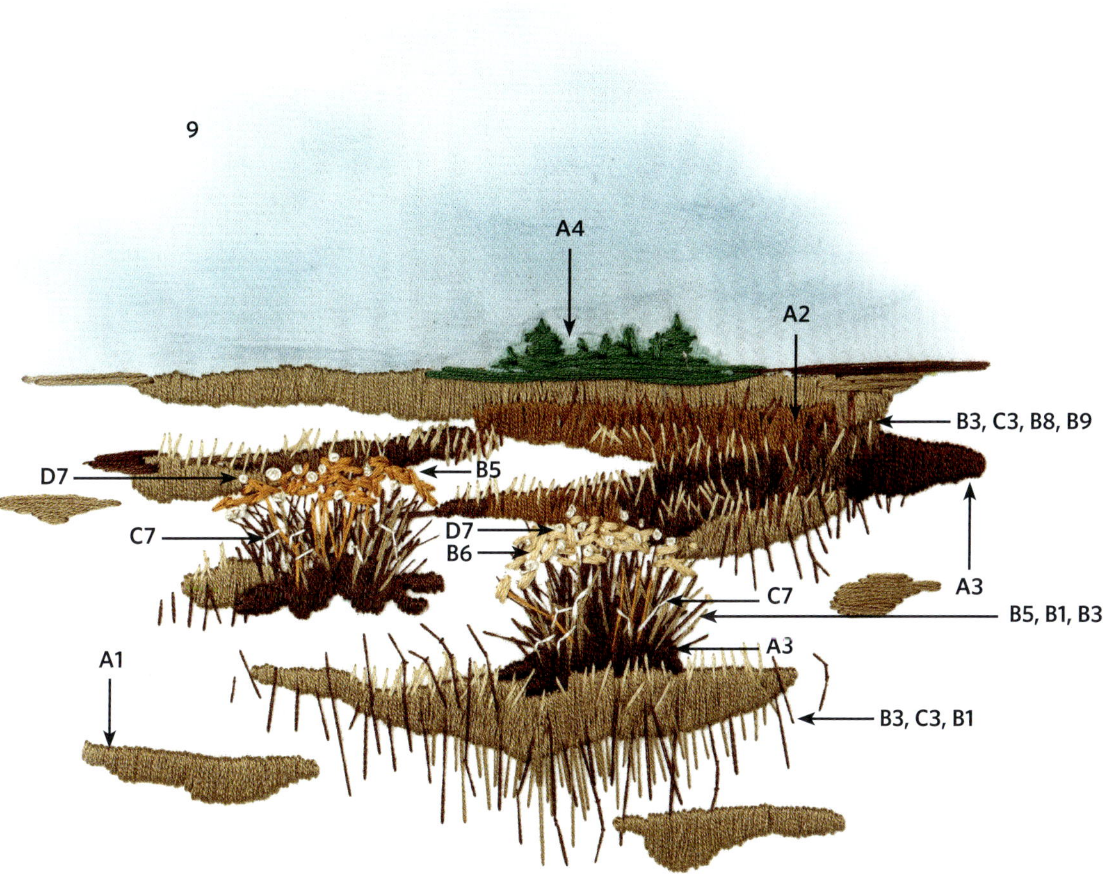
9
A4
A2
B3, C3, B8, B9
D7
B5
C7
D7
B6
A3
C7
B5, B1, B3
A3
A1
B3, C3, B1

## PATTERN

Enlarge 150%

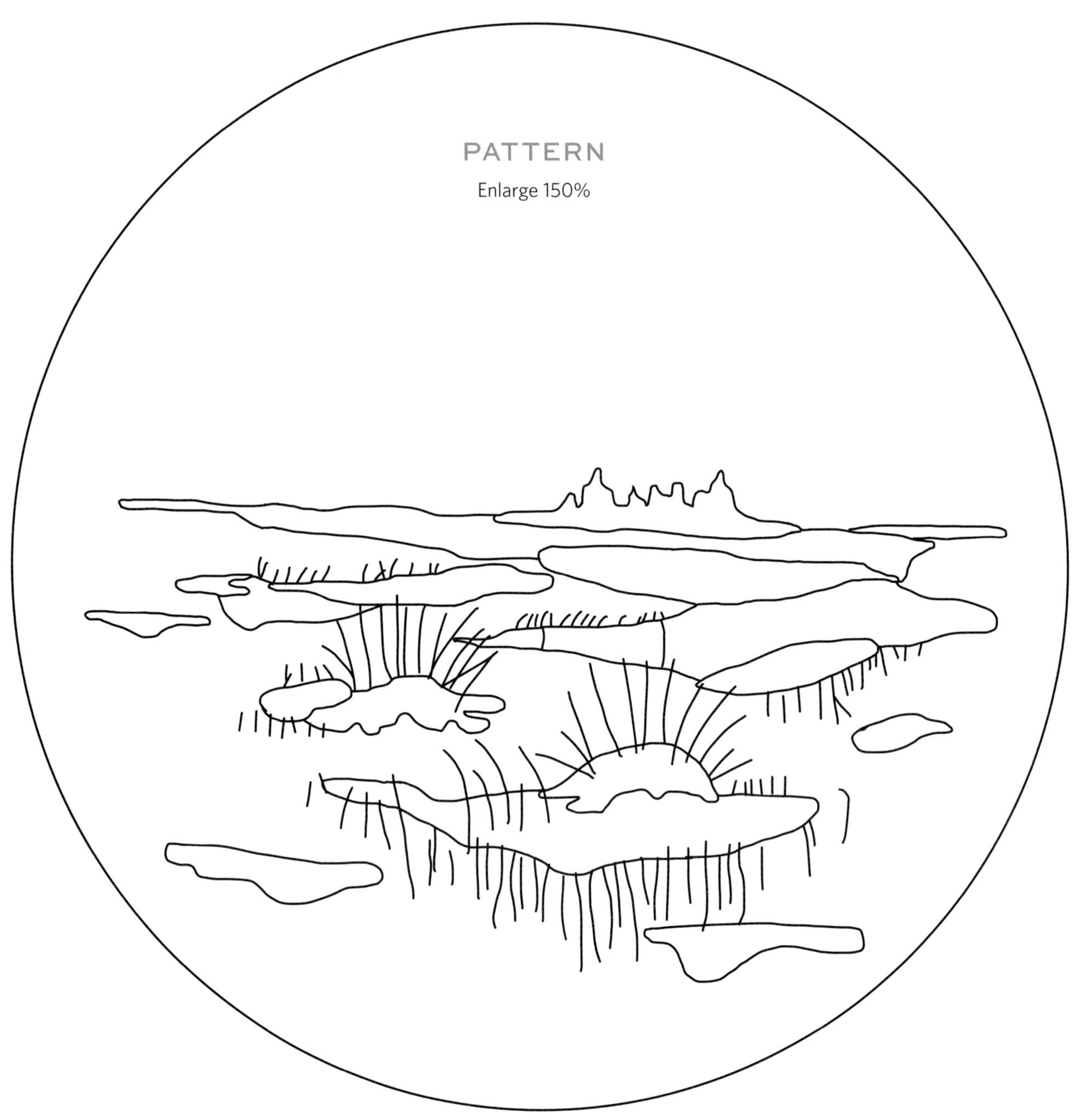

## Creating Perspective

Perspective is the art of drawing—or stitching—on a two-dimensional surface in a way that creates realistic spatial relationships between objects. In a landscape scene, perspective creates an appearance of spatial distance even though the surface is flat. There are two types of perspective in art: linear perspective (using a vanishing point on the horizon and making lines that converge at that point) and atmospheric perspective (making objects look like they are fading into the background). I mainly use atmospheric perspective in my work. To do this I try to make the stitches in my foreground as detailed and large as possible while making the stitching near the horizon line smaller and less detailed.

Linear perspective

Atmospheric perspective

## Transfer the Pattern

Using a water-soluble fabric marker, transfer the pattern onto the cloth.

## Stitch the Middle Ground

Fill each section of brown grass with six-strand satin stitches. Use color 611 for the lightest grass, 869 for the midtone grass, and 801 for the darkest grass.

## Stitch the Background

Use six-strand horizontal satin stitches in color 520 for the tree line. The stitches at the tops of the trees will be much shorter than the stitches that form the base. We will come back to paint the sky at the very end.

## Stitch the Foreground

To add the dead rabbitbrush, first satin stitch a mound in color 801 using six strands. From that base, extend two-strand straight stitches 1"–2" long in all directions for the stems in colors 801, 782, and 611. Stitch with the darkest dark first, shift to your midtone, and finish with the lightest color.

Create the top of the rabbitbrush with small six-strand straight stitches. Use color 422 for the foremost rabbitbrush and 782 for the one farther back. You generally want to orient these stitches horizontally on top of the stems, but be sure to use a variety of stitch lengths and directions to make it look organic. Next, create French knots in color 613 on top of the straight stitches.

Use a two-strand couched straight stitch in your lightest light color (613) to add a few pieces of bent grass to each rabbitbrush, which will make the plants look realistic and draw attention to them.

Finally, layer grass on top of your satin-stitched areas with two-strand straight stitches

Stitch the rabbitbrush one layer at a time.

and couched straight stitches in colors 801, 611, 612, and 433. Leave the area nearest the horizon line free of any detail to create atmospheric perspective and a sense of depth.

## Run the Hoop Under Water

Run the entire hoop under hot water to wash out the pattern transfer marks and tighten your fabric. Let it dry before painting.

## Paint with Watercolor

Make sure you practice on scrap fabric before you apply paint to your final project! Wet the entire area of the fabric above the horizon line with a clean paintbrush and water. Now mix your paint: Add a small dab of black to the cerulean blue. Clean the paintbrush in a container of water. The colored water in the container is what we'll paint with, because we want a really faint color in the sky. Add a dab of tinted water to four or five spots in the sky, letting it bleed across the fabric.

## Finish the Hoop

Refer to Finishing Your Embroidery (page 56).

### All About Layers

Layers create depth and visual interest to landscape embroidery. There are countless ways to introduce depth by layering materials, compositional elements, and even the stitches themselves.

# SPRING

*It is sometimes so bitterly cold in the winter that one says, 'The cold is too awful for me to care whether summer is coming or not; the harm outdoes the good.' But with or without our approval, the severe weather does come to an end eventually and one fine morning the wind changes and there is the thaw.*

—Vincent van Gogh

Picture the moment you throw your windows open after a long winter. Your body feels the first warmth. A fresh smell replaces stale air. You hear birds chirping. What beautiful relief. I wait all year for this moment, and I'm always struck that it would never feel so sweet if winter hadn't felt so long.

With our spring landscape, we build on what we learned in winter by adding wool roving to the fabric and working with more color. We will layer stitches and materials to add complexity to the textures of the field.

## MY DESIGN PROCESS

Spring catches our attention because of its brilliant greens, but there is still a lot of brown in the landscape. I've honestly never liked how brown and green look together, but I committed to keeping this hoop true to the essence of spring. To capture the feel of the season, I also chose cooler greens compared to what I use in the summer piece.

In addition to sketching a landscape, I recommend taking some photos. Keep those photos close by as you work, so you can refer to the general color structure of the land. I had the photo in front of me on a computer screen as I stitched, holding the hoop up to the image every time I added a new color. Looking at the photo repeatedly, I noticed how the colors closest to the horizon line were much lighter than the ones directly in the foreground.

I mirrored this effect in my thread colors, with the lightest satin stitching at the top of the middle ground and the darkest at the bottom.

Refer back to the original photo on page 76 (upper right corner) and you'll notice that I edited the landscape. At the horizon line in the photo, there are some light green trees in front of the dark evergreens. I decided to omit the lighter trees because I wanted to create a part of the composition that was quieter than all the rest. If there is a lot of detail everywhere, the composition is static. When you leave part of it emptier, the eye can travel around the entire piece.

## COLOR AND STITCH GUIDE

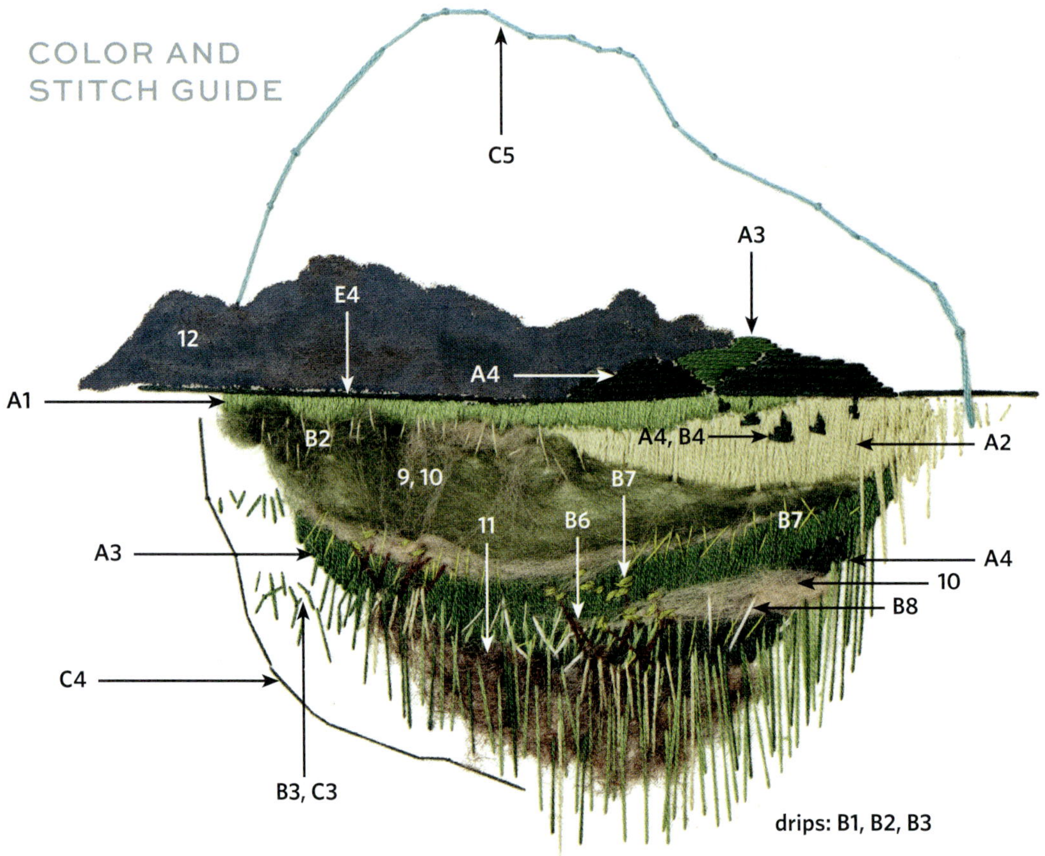

| CODE LETTER | STITCHES |
|---|---|
| **A** | Satin stitch |
| **B** | Straight stitch |
| **C** | Couched straight stitch |
| **E** | Backstitch |

| CODE NUMBER | WISTYRIA WOOL ROVING COLORS |
|---|---|
| **9** | Forest green |
| **10** | Camel |
| **11** | Medium gray |

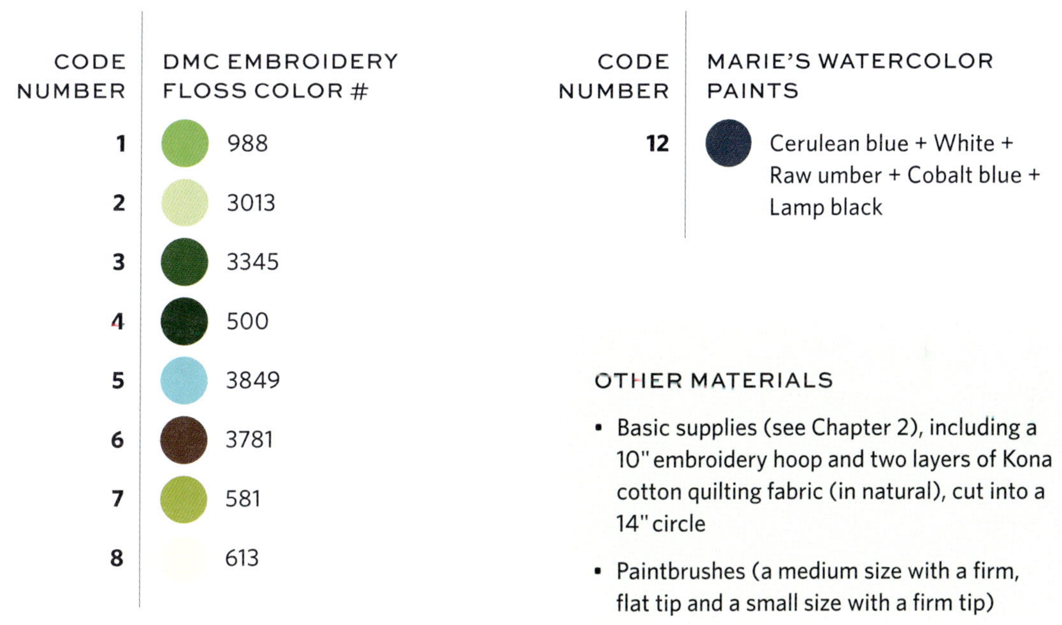

| CODE NUMBER | DMC EMBROIDERY FLOSS COLOR # |
|---|---|
| **1** | 988 |
| **2** | 3013 |
| **3** | 3345 |
| **4** | 500 |
| **5** | 3849 |
| **6** | 3781 |
| **7** | 581 |
| **8** | 613 |

| CODE NUMBER | MARIE'S WATERCOLOR PAINTS |
|---|---|
| **12** | Cerulean blue + White + Raw umber + Cobalt blue + Lamp black |

## OTHER MATERIALS

- Basic supplies (see Chapter 2), including a 10" embroidery hoop and two layers of Kona cotton quilting fabric (in natural), cut into a 14" circle
- Paintbrushes (a medium size with a firm, flat tip and a small size with a firm tip)

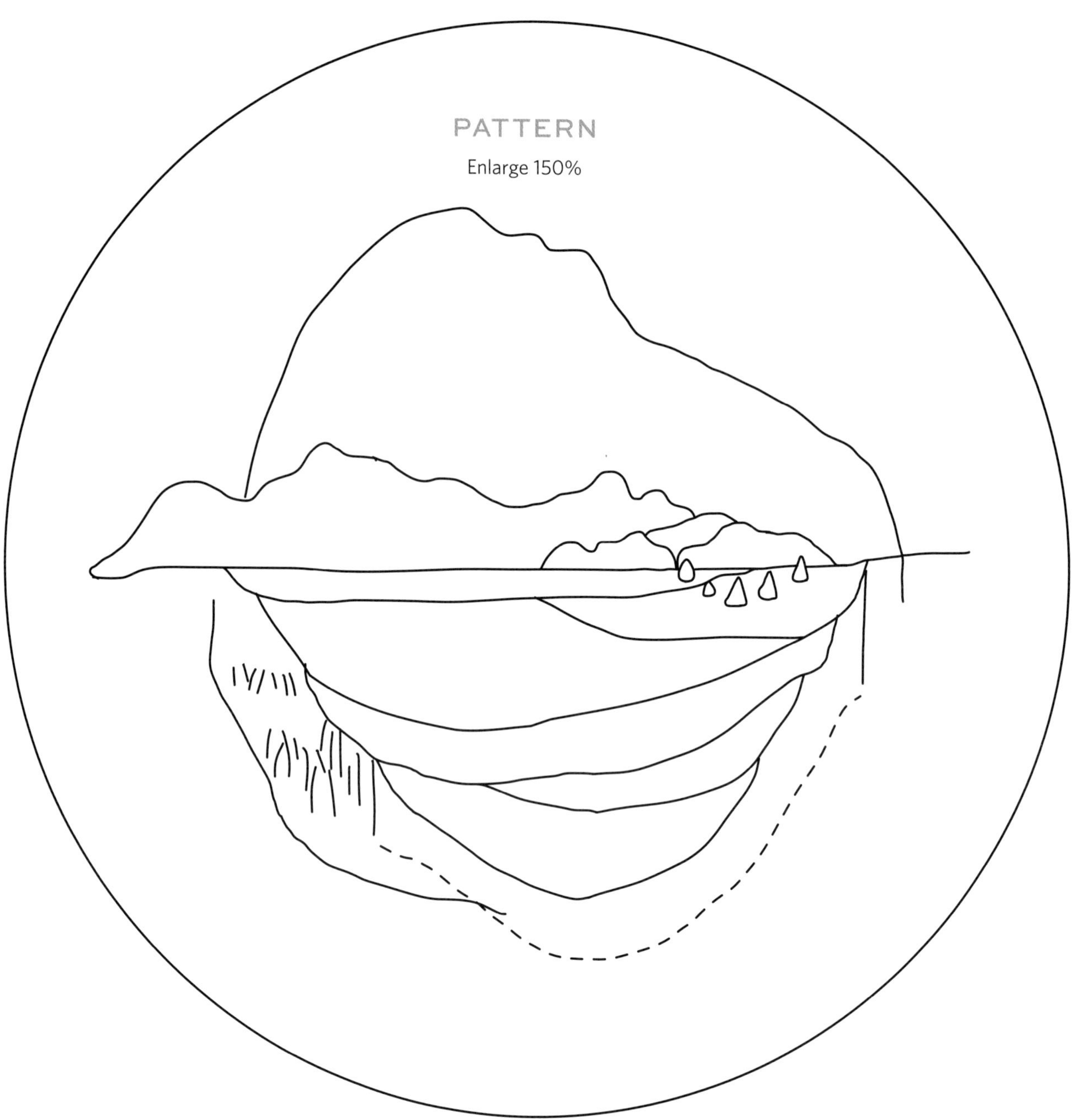

## PATTERN

Enlarge 150%

## Transfer the Pattern

Using a heat-erasable pen, transfer the pattern onto the cloth.

## Stitch the Middle Ground

Use a six-strand satin stitch to fill the two sections of the field closest to the horizon line with colors 988 and 3013.

In the area below the satin stitching, lay down some forest green wool roving and spread a thin layer of camel-colored wool over it, creating subtlety in the colors of your field. Always use a little more than you think you need. Anchor the roving with eight stitches that extend from the satin-stitched area into the top edge of the wool, using six strands of colors 988 and 3013. To seal in the wool roving, satin stitch a section directly below the wool with six strands of color 3345, catching the bottom edge of the wool as you finish each stitch.

Fill the lowest satin-stitched section with six-strand floss in color 500.

Below that, add medium gray wool roving. Attach with two-strand straight stitches that create drips directly over and into the wool in colors 988, 3013, and 3345.

### Painting with Wool

As you satin stitch around wool roving, the wool often pulls in directions you don't want. Use your needle to tease the wool back in shape. I find I need to do this several times throughout the creation of the piece.

## Stitch the Background

Use a six-strand couched straight stitch in color 3849 to create the shape of the sky.

Use a six-strand satin stitch to fill in the tree line with colors 500 and 3345. These stitches are horizontal and will be about 1" long at the base. With such long stitches, take care not to pull tightly and pucker the fabric.

Add the dark horizon line with a six-strand backstitch in color 500.

## Paint with Watercolor

Make sure you practice on scrap fabric before you apply paint to your final piece! Note that we are working with the dry method of watercolor for this project by not getting the fabric wet before we add paint.

Mix equal parts cerulean blue, white, raw umber, and cobalt blue. Add a tiny dab of black and mix well. Add enough water that the paint loosens, but not so much that it becomes watery. Using a medium-size brush with a flat, firm top for the inside of the mountains and a small, firm brush for the edges, paint the mountains. Let dry before moving on.

## Stitch the Foreground and Details

You won't be able to see pattern markings for grasses and plants layered over the middle ground, so you'll need to improvise those stitches.

For the outer line at the left edge, use a two-strand couched straight stitch in color 500.

Add the branches of the rabbitbrush bushes with several two-strand straight stitches in color 3781. Switching colors, use small six-strand straight stitches to add leaves at the top of the rabbitbrush in color 581.

Use single-strand straight stitches in color 581 for the grass along the bottom of the forest green and camel-colored wool section. Switching to color 3013, use single-strand straight stitches for the grass at the top of the same section.

For the small trees below the horizon line, use six-strand floss in color 500. The bottom of each tree is two or three horizontal satin stitches. Use a vertical straight stitch to create the point.

Lay a tiny bit of camel-colored wool roving at the top edge of the bottom satin-stitched section. Use a few two-strand straight stitches in color 613 to attach the wool and add grass to the left of the wool you just added.

Use two-strand straight stitches in color 3345 to add grass between the outer line and middle ground. Curve a few of those grass blades with a couched straight stitch.

Add drips to the lightest satin-stitched section on the right side of the landscape and the horizon line with six-strand straight stitches in colors 988, 3013, and 3345.

## Finish the Hoop

Use a hair dryer to remove any residual markings. Refer to Finishing Your Embroidery (page 56).

# SUMMER

*I meant to do my work today—*
*But a brown bird sang in the apple tree,*
*And a butterfly flitted across the field,*
*And all the leaves were calling me.*

—Richard Le Gallienne

The ease of summer is in its beauty. Everywhere you look there are flowers blooming, birds flitting, fields growing green. Inspiration is everywhere, and yet I often struggle to make landscape pieces in summer. Maybe there is simply too much life and so much beauty that finding one subtlety to spark my imagination is harder. Or maybe I'm drawn more to work in my garden than in my studio. Whatever the reason, I hold the lull in my embroidery practice loosely. In summer I am soaking up inspiration from the land, remaining present to its beauty, even when I'm not in the studio as much.

With this piece, we'll layer additional techniques to our practice, using fabric collage and thread drips.

## MY DESIGN PROCESS

I created this piece in fall by looking at a photo taken in summer (see page 76, bottom left). While sketching and first stitching, I studied the photo to decide where I wanted the different textures and patches of grass. Once well underway, though, I stopped looking at the photograph and studied the hoop itself to see if things were working well. At some point during the process, you need to let go of the actual landscape that inspired you and turn your attention to the composition inside the hoop. Is there movement? Do the colors work together? Is there a clear focal point? Don't hesitate to improvise elements that weren't in the original scene if they help the composition.

Early in the design process, I knew I wanted the yellow thread to be my focal point—the area that would catch the eye first and the color that could move the eye around the hoop. Once I'd stitched my middle ground and the drips, I added bright yellow flowers and a few yellow streaks to the drips, but immediately I could tell something wasn't working. The yellow was so bright, and I'd used too much, so the composition had no clear starting point. Cutting out the yellow drips solved the problem.

## COLOR AND STITCH GUIDE

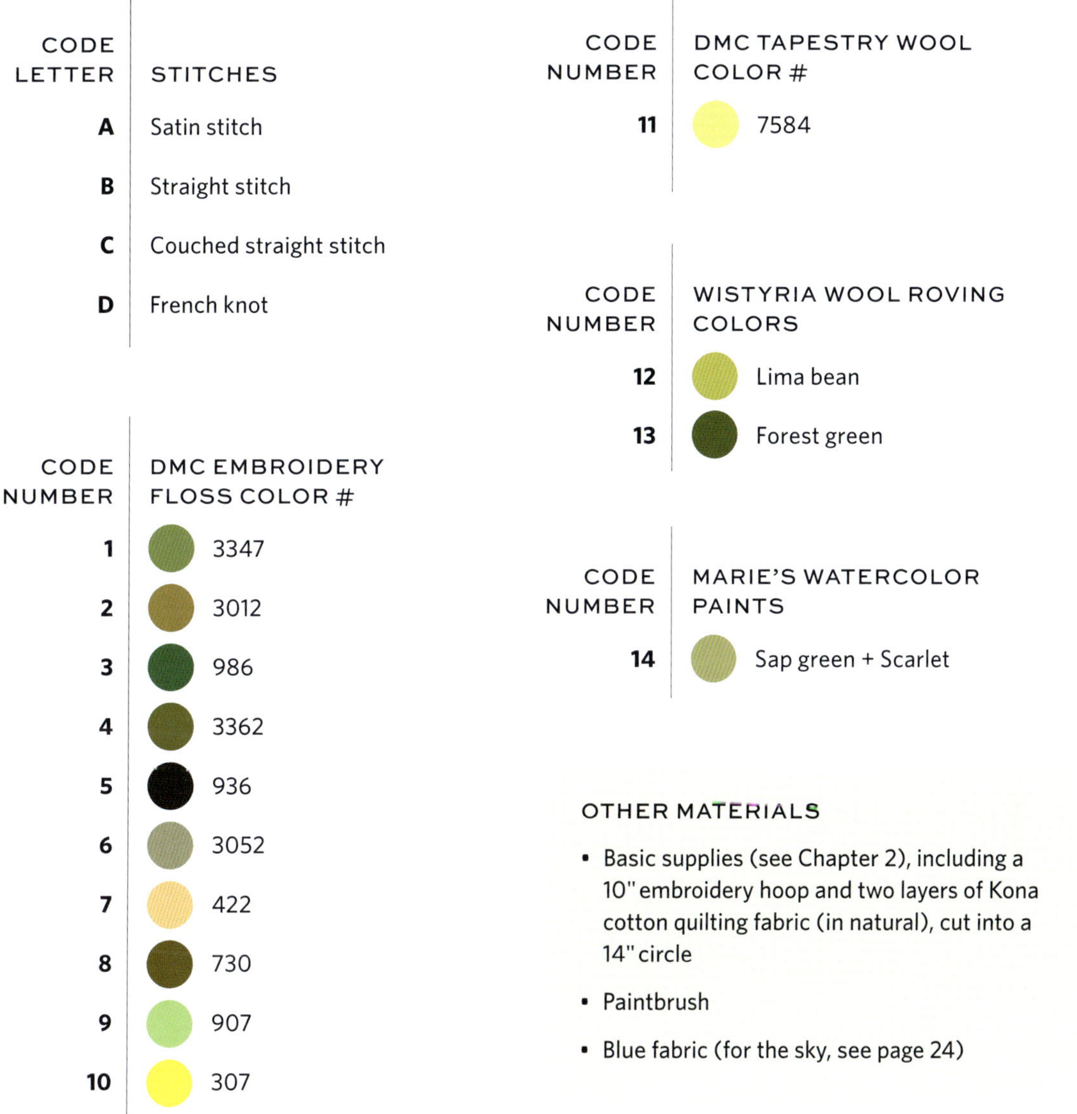

| CODE LETTER | STITCHES |
|---|---|
| **A** | Satin stitch |
| **B** | Straight stitch |
| **C** | Couched straight stitch |
| **D** | French knot |

| CODE NUMBER | DMC EMBROIDERY FLOSS COLOR # |
|---|---|
| **1** | 3347 |
| **2** | 3012 |
| **3** | 986 |
| **4** | 3362 |
| **5** | 936 |
| **6** | 3052 |
| **7** | 422 |
| **8** | 730 |
| **9** | 907 |
| **10** | 307 |

| CODE NUMBER | DMC TAPESTRY WOOL COLOR # |
|---|---|
| **11** | 7584 |

| CODE NUMBER | WISTYRIA WOOL ROVING COLORS |
|---|---|
| **12** | Lima bean |
| **13** | Forest green |

| CODE NUMBER | MARIE'S WATERCOLOR PAINTS |
|---|---|
| **14** | Sap green + Scarlet |

### OTHER MATERIALS

- Basic supplies (see Chapter 2), including a 10" embroidery hoop and two layers of Kona cotton quilting fabric (in natural), cut into a 14" circle
- Paintbrush
- Blue fabric (for the sky, see page 24)

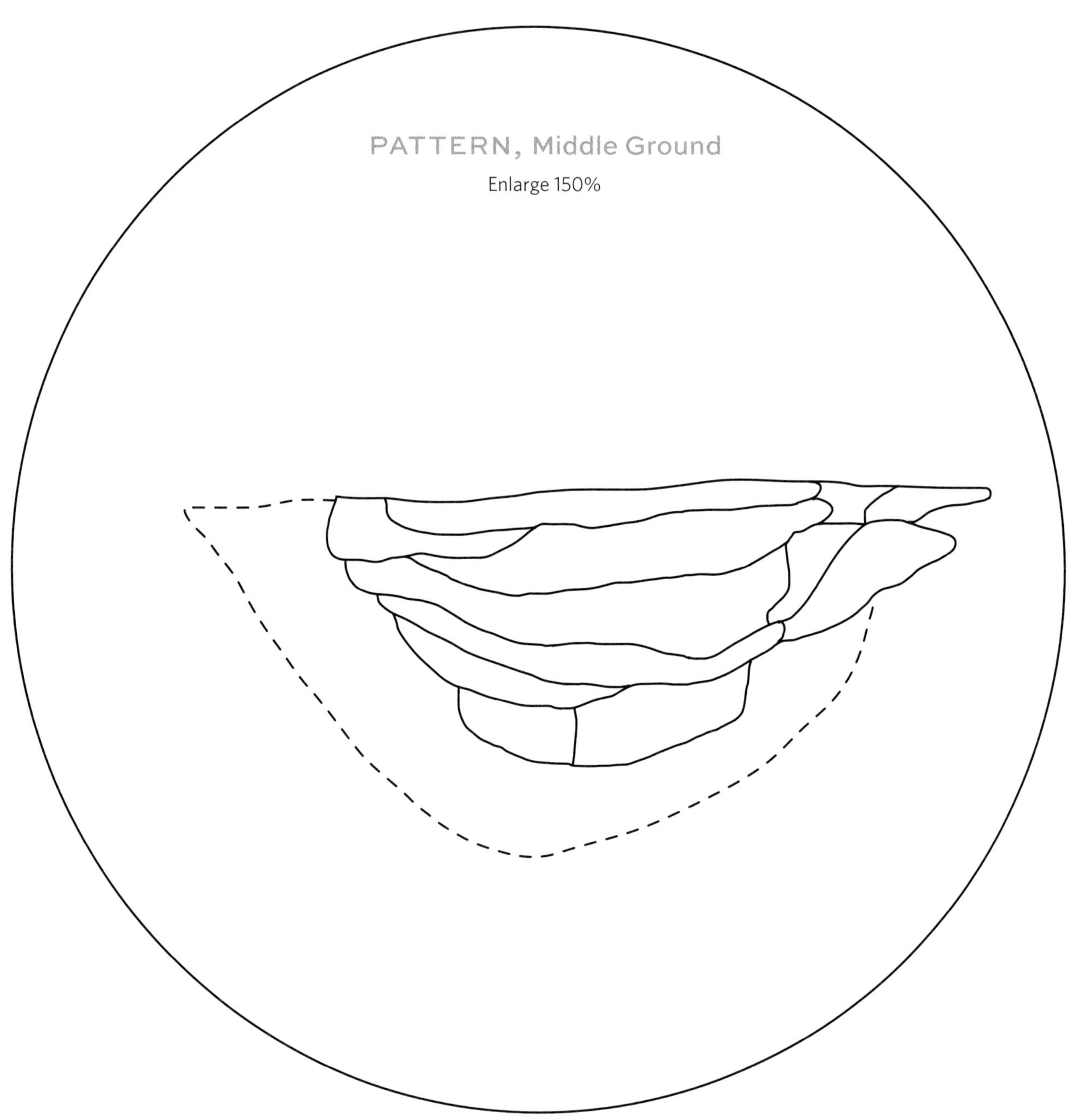
PATTERN, Middle Ground
Enlarge 150%

Foreground details will conceal much of the middle ground. Layering stitches and textures is an important part of suggesting the depth and complexity of a landscape.

PATTERN,
Foreground and Background
Enlarge 150%

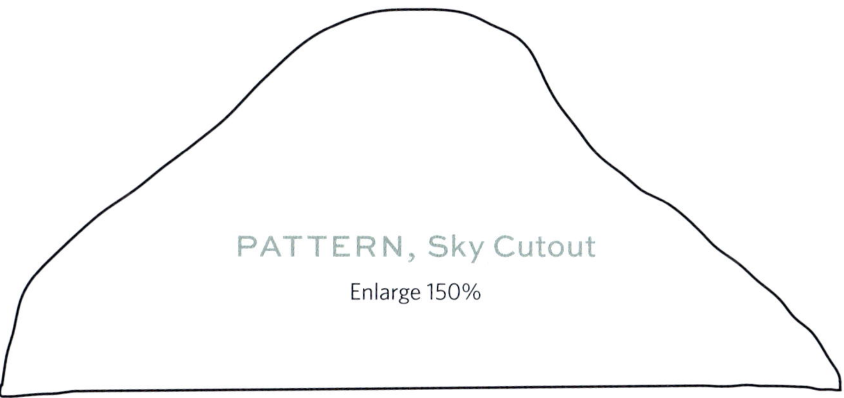


## Transfer the Pattern

Using a water-soluble fabric marker, transfer the pattern for the middle ground (see page 100) onto the cloth.

## Stitch the Middle Ground

Use a six-strand satin stitch to fill the top sections of the field closest to the horizon line with colors 3347 and 3012. Use six strands of 3012 and two strands of tapesty wool in color 7584 to fill in the horizontal satin-stitched area on the right side of the horizon line.

In an area below the vertical satin stitching, lay down some lima bean wool roving. Always use a little more than you think you need. Anchor the roving with six stitches in color 3347 and 3012 that extend from the satin-stitched area into the top edge of the wool. To seal in the wool roving, satin stitch a section directly below the wool using six strands of 986 and 3362, catching the bottom edge of the wool as you finish each stitch.

Continue to fill all the satin-stitched sections with six-strand floss in colors 936 and 3362. When you reach the section of forest green wool roving near the bottom of the composition, attach it in the same way, securing it above with a few stitches in color 3362 and with satin stitching below in colors 3052 and 3012.

## Run the Hoop Under Water

Run the entire hoop under hot water to wash out the pattern transfer marks and tighten your fabric. Let it dry before painting.

## Paint with Watercolor

I'm going to remind you every time: Make sure you practice on scrap fabric before you apply paint to your final piece! Note that we are working with the dry method of watercolor for this project by not getting the fabric wet before we add paint.

Mix 10 parts sap green to 1 part scarlet. Soak your brush with water and pick up some paint. You don't want the paint to be thick, so soaking the brush helps. Refer to page 101 and paint the area you want colored. Let dry before moving on.

## Transfer the Next Pattern

Using a heat-erasable pen, draw what you can from the second pattern layer (page 102) onto the middle ground. You won't be able to mark some of the foreground details, so you will have to eyeball that as you stitch.

### Vary the Direction of Satin Stitches

One of my favorite tricks in landscape embroidery is to mix vertical satin stitching with a few interspersed patches of horizontal satin stitching. The horizontal stitching amplifies perspective by emphasizing the flatness of the field as it recedes in space. This technique also adds a realistic variation in texture.

## Stitch the Background

Using the pattern on page 103, cut the sky from blue fabric and attach it to the base fabric with double-sided tape.

Use a six-strand horizontal satin stitch to fill in the tree line in color 936. Use six-strand straight stitches going vertically to create the points of a few of the trees.

Use two-strand couched straight stitches to create the shape of the mountains in color 936.

Using tapestry wool in color 7584, add a few satin stitches about 3" long at the base of the blue fabric to bring the field up to the horizon line and further secure the collaged fabric.

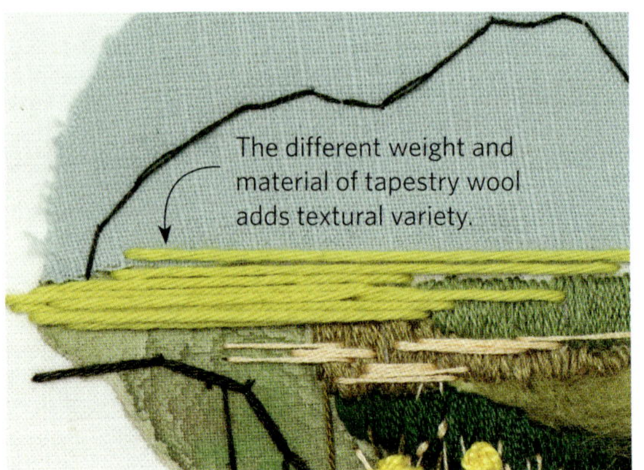

## Stitch the Foreground and Drips

Use a two-strand horizontal satin stitch in color 422 to add tan patches of grass toward the top of the middle ground. Add more tan grass near the base of the middle ground with lines of vertical straight stitches using two strands of color 422.

Use a heat-erasable pen to map out the drip area on top of the watercolor.

Use a six-strand couched straight stitch to create the dark green line at the base of the middle ground in color 936.

Use two-strand straight stitches 1"–2" long to create the drips. (See Thread Drips on page 71.) Start with the midtone colors and end with your darkest dark, using colors 907, 422, 730, 936.

To create grass and seed heads on top of the drips, add two-strand straight stitches as well as two-strand French knots wrapped two or three times around the needle in color 907.

For the yellow flowers, use a six-strand satin stitch as well as six-strand French knots wrapped two to four times around the needle in color 307. Add a few four-strand horizontal satin stitches to suggest the flower patches in the back of the field.

## Finish the Hoop

Use a hair dryer to remove any residual markings. Refer to Finishing Your Embroidery (page 56).

# FALL

*I came to see myself as growing out of the earth like the other native animals and plants. I saw my body and my daily motions as brief coherences and articulations of the energy of the place, which would fall back into it like leaves in the autumn.*

—Wendell Berry

Spring's verdant greens still shine in the midline of blades of grass, while winter's browns creep across fading plants and leaves. Some of summer's flowers are dying, and some—like the California poppy—are still blooming strong, waiting for the first hard frost. Fall is the place where all seasons meet. What a perfect place to end our seasonal journey through this field.

Take a moment to note what you've learned since you began with the winter scene. The fall landscape will be a celebration of technique and of color—embroidery floss, wool, fabric, watercolor all richly layered and woven together to create a moody field dotted with bright yellow rabbitbrush.

## MY DESIGN PROCESS

This piece was very challenging for me. I had such high expectations, wanting it to be the culmination of all our techniques and seasons. I spent hours stitching, following the plan in my head and the one laid out in my sketchbook and referencing the original inspiration image (see page 76, bottom right). I just didn't like how it looked! I tried my usual method of taking a photo and editing the composition with my paint tool, but I felt stuck, and my confidence spiraled. I put the hoop in a drawer and didn't look at it for two months. To my great surprise and relief, when I returned to it with fresh eyes, I knew the composition just needed a little more negative space in the field, which was easily achieved with a few sections of wool roving.

When you feel stuck and frustrated—and everyone does sometimes—stepping away is okay. I have done this many times. Sometimes I pick the piece up again a few months later and know exactly what it needs. Other times I pick it up and still can't figure out what's wrong, in which case I may walk away from it forever. The process of starting a creative project is worthwhile even if you never finish.

| CODE LETTER | STITCHES |
|---|---|
| **A** | Satin stitch |
| **B** | Straight stitch |

| CODE NUMBER | DMC EMBROIDERY FLOSS COLOR # |
|---|---|
| **1** | 372 |
| **2** | 420 |
| **3** | 840 |
| **4** | 838 |
| **5** | 680 |
| **6** | 613 |
| **7** | 520 |
| **8** | 726 |

| CODE NUMBER | WISTYRIA WOOL ROVING COLORS |
|---|---|
| **9** | Camel |
| **10** | Butterscotch |
| **11** | Toffee |
| **12** | Chocolate |
| **13** | Medium gray |

| CODE NUMBER | MARIE'S WATERCOLOR PAINTS |
|---|---|
| **13** | Prussian blue + Gamboge + White |

### OTHER MATERIALS

- Basic supplies (see Chapter 2), including a 10" embroidery hoop and two layers of Kona cotton quilting fabric (in natural), cut into a 14" circle
- Paintbrush
- Blue fabric (for the sky, see page 24)

## COLOR AND STITCH GUIDE

PATTERN

Enlarge 150%

## Transfer the Pattern

Using a water-soluble fabric marker, transfer the pattern onto the cloth.

## Stitch the Middle Ground

Use a six-strand satin stitch to fill the top sections of the field closest to the horizon line. Make vertical satin stitches in colors 840, 420, and 372. Add a few horizontal satin stitches in 838 on the far right side. Then add the horizontal satin stitches that create the horizon line in color 372.

In an area below the satin stitching, lay down some camel-colored wool roving, referring to the image above for placement. Always use a little more than you think you need. Anchor the roving with six stitches that extend from the satin-stitched area into the top edge of the wool. To seal in the wool roving, satin stitch a section directly below the wool, using six strands of color 680. Catch the bottom edge of the wool as you finish each stitch.

The rest of the wool roving is attached with a different method. Lay out the toffee, butterscotch, and chocolate wool, using the hoop on page 111 for reference. With three or four ½" straight stitches approximately every inch, anchor the wool with two strands of embroidery floss in matching colors: 420 on the toffee wool, 680 on the butterscotch wool, and 838 on the chocolate wool.

Add some grass on top of the wool using a few long two-strand straight stitches with flosses 372 and 680. These initial stitches are to anchor the wool, so use just enough to keep it in place. You'll add additional layers of grass when you stitch the foreground.

Spread a small amount of medium gray wool below the chocolate wool. Secure in place using approximately thirty 1" single-strand straight stitches with floss 613. Your stitches should extend into the chocolate wool, further anchoring that roving.

Using flosses 838 and 680, create drips at the bottom of the piece with with two-strand straight stitches 1"–2" long that primarily cover a portion of the chocolate wool. Fade the drips away as you move from left to right, leaving a portion of the wool unstitched at the bottom edge.

## Run the Hoop Under Water

Run your entire hoop under hot water to wash out the pattern transfer marks and tighten your fabric. Let it dry before continuing.

## Stitch the Background

Using a heat-erasable pen, draw or re-transfer the remaining elements of the pattern onto the background. You won't be able to mark the foreground details, so you'll have to eyeball those when you stitch them.

Cut the sky from blue fabric and attach it to the base fabric with double-sided tape.

Using floss 372, add a few more horizontal six-strand straight stitches at the base of the blue fabric to further secure it.

Use a six-strand satin stitch to fill in the tree line in color 520. Use a few six-strand straight stitches going vertically to create the points of a few of the trees.

## Paint with Watercolor

Make sure you practice on scrap fabric before you apply paint to your final piece! Mix three parts Prussian blue with one part gamboge. Add a few dabs of white to lighten the color. Add just enough water to the paint so that it's easy to spread but doesn't bleed.

Using the dry method (see page 65), fill in the mountains with paint.

Let the fabric dry completely before moving on to the foreground.

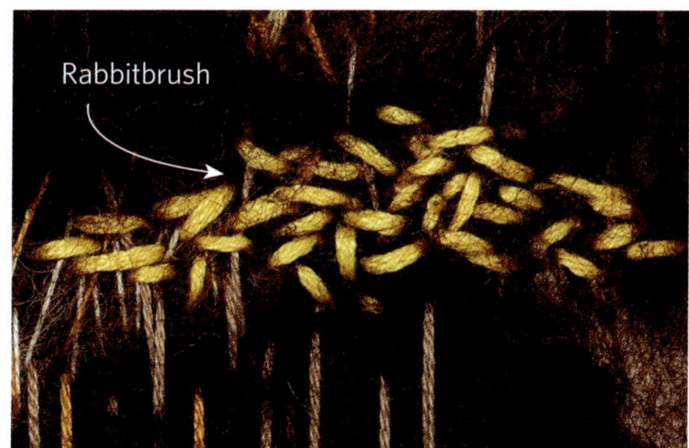


## Stitch the Foreground

Stitch the rabbitbrush using a series of small six-strand straight stitches with floss 726. Vary the direction of the stitches, with most oriented horizontally and a few vertically.

Using colors 680 and 372, add grasses to the middle ground where indicated on the pattern. In general, use two-strand straight stitches in the back of the field and single-strand straight stitches in the foreground.

Add a few more six-strand satin stitches in floss 520 just under the patch of trees.

Evaluate the composition and add any more drips or grasses that you may need.

Use a needle to brush out the exposed wool, nudging it into place. You can also pull out or trim excess wool at this point.

### What If I Need to Add More Wool?

Often I remove some wool from a section and take too much. Thankfully there is an easy fix. Add a bit more wool back, securing it with a few straight stitches on top. Depending on the color you use, these straight stitches could look like grass on top of the wool or they could match and disappear.

## Finish the Hoop

Use a hair dryer to remove any residual markings. Refer to Finishing Your Embroidery (page 56).

CHAPTER 6

# BUILDING BLOCKS OF A LANDSCAPE

There was a season in my life when I didn't have the time, space, and inspiration for art making as I had previously known it in the mediums of drawing and sculpture. Without any goal in mind other than to continue creating, I stitched—or sketched—countless nature studies, which later became the foundations of my embroidered landscapes.

While I encourage you to study nature firsthand and interpret it in your own way with needle and thread, I'm also delighted to share a collection of embroidered natural motifs for you to borrow and adapt. These middle-ground and background elements, as well as foreground details such as flowers and grasses, are building blocks for you to use in creating your own original landscapes. You will need to adjust their scale to work for your specific embroidery, but I have included the stitches and floss colors as jumping-off points. Find transfer patterns for the flowers and plants on pages 196–199. The middle ground elements on the following pages don't require a particular template but are designed to be adapted to any landscape that inspires you. There are also projects in Chapter 7 that assemble the building blocks into finished compositions.

# MIDDLE GROUNDS

## BASIC GRASS FIELD

This building block is a basic green field over which you can layer foreground details. Use satin stitching to lay down a base color, and then add straight stitches on top to blend the satin-stitched base and create a grasslike texture.

- DMC embroidery floss: 907, 935, 3011, 3052
- Six-strand satin stitch, two-strand straight stitch

## The Meaning of Plants

We cultivate a connection to the land by assigning meaning to certain plants. Our histories are woven together in the stories we tell about what different plants symbolize. Considering the meaning of a plant as you design an embroidered landscape can deepen the richness and symbolic meaning of your work.

- **BLACK-EYED SUSAN:** encouragement
- **BLUE SPRUCE:** eternal life, protection, and healing
- **CRASPEDIA:** good health
- **CONEFLOWER:** health and wellness
- **DANDELION:** resilience and strength
- **GOLDENROD:** wholeness
- **LAVENDER:** serenity and calmness
- **MILKWEED:** hope and resilience
- **OAK TREE:** strength, resilience, and endurance
- **ORIENTAL POPPY:** remembrance
- **SALVIA:** health
- **SUNFLOWER:** happiness
- **THISTLE:** devotion, bravery, and strength

Craspedia

Coneflower

Oriental Poppy

## DRIED FIELD

Essentially this is a brown version of the basic grass field on page 116—it uses the same method of laying down a satin-stitch base and then creating grass texture with straight stitches. For textural variation, leave open spaces of satin stitches with no straight stitching on top.

- DMC embroidery floss: 613, 832, 869, 3781, 3828
- Six-strand satin stitch, two-strand straight stitch

## PATCHWORK GRASS FIELD

Combine wool roving with satin stitching for a patchwork effect. Create visual interest by adding a few straight stitches. This type of middle ground works great for an abstract representation of a field. You can make it more realistic depending on the foreground details you add.

- Wistyria wool roving: forest green
- DMC embroidery floss: 905, 935, 3052
- DMC tapestry wool: 7584
- Six-strand satin stitch, wool roving, and two-strand straight stitch

## PATCHWORK DRIED FIELD

This brown version of the patchwork grass field shows how the effect will vary depending on where you place the wool and satin stitches in relation to each other. This building block is a great base for a fall or winter landscape.

- Wistyria wool roving: camel
- DMC embroidery floss: 613, 844, 869, 3032, 3781
- Six-strand satin stitch, wool roving, and two-strand straight stitch

## PATCHWORK GRASS WITH WATERCOLOR

This building block demonstrates how you can add watercolor as part of the middle ground. The watercolor hue can be as saturated as you want. When planning foreground details, keep in mind that watercolor is harder to stitch on.

- Wistyria wool roving: fir
- DMC embroidery floss: 163, 832, 935, 3347
- Marie's watercolor paints: sap green, scarlet
- Six-strand satin stitch, wool roving, and watercolor paint on wet fabric

## OUTLINED SKY

Sometimes I want to create a circular composition, but a dry-painted sky feels too heavy. Outlining the sky works well because stitches don't have as much weight.

- Two-strand couched straight stitch in any color of the sky

## OUTLINED MOUNTAINS

These mountains are a simple way to add line work that guides the eye along the horizon line. They add a bit of visual interest but aren't as weighty as the painted mountains.

- Two-strand couched straight stitch in any color of the mountains

## FABRIC-COLLAGE SKY

This sky is a simple but dramatic addition to your landscape and can be added at any point after you've stitched your middle ground. I've used blue fabric, but use any color you want.

- See Fabric Collage (page 69).

## PAINTED MOUNTAINS

Painted mountains add weight to the top of your horizon line—especially helpful if your composition feels bottom heavy and needs balance.

- See Painting on Dry Fabric (page 65).

## WET-PAINTED SKY

Adding a gradient of watercolor above the horizon line creates an open feeling at the top of the composition, subtly adding color and suggesting a sky.

- See Painting on Wet Fabric (page 63).

## DRY-PAINTED SKY

Painting on dry fabric creates a more solid boundary for the sky. I tend to create circular compositions, and this method works well for keeping the eye within that circle and moving it over the landscape.

- See Painting on Dry Fabric (page 65).

## BACHELOR'S BUTTON

*Centaurea cyanus*

Another name for bachelor's button is cornflower, because these plants have been frequent weeds in cornfields. Due to their particularly bright colors—blue, purple, white, or pink—these flowers are a great tool for leading the eye around a landscape composition.

- DMC embroidery floss: 31, 154, 341, 988
- Two- to four-strand straight stitch for the petals and leaves
- Two-strand couched straight stitch for the stem
- Four-strand satin stitch for the bud
- French knot for the flower center with two-strand floss wrapped four times around the needle

## BLACK-EYED SUSAN

*Rudbeckia hirta*

These wildflowers are known as pioneer plants because they are always one of the first to grow in burned or damaged environments. With petals in a deep yellow that sometimes approaches orange, black-eyed Susans are darker than many other yellow flowers. I often add them to a landscape when I want a yellow for my color palette that isn't too bright.

- DMC embroidery floss: 444, 728, 938, 988
- Six-strand satin stitch for the flower's center
- Four-strand straight stitch for the petals and leaves
- Four-strand couched straight stitch for the stem

## BLUE FLAX

*Linum lewisii*

Flax is a versatile and utilitarian plant: Its fibers make linen, its oils make linseed oil, and you can eat its nutritious seeds. I find myself using blue flax often in my landscapes because its broad-petaled flowers stand out well against a dark green middle ground.

- DMC embroidery floss: 341, 445, 844, 3053
- Six-strand satin stitch for the petals
- French knot for the flower center and seed heads, with two-strand floss wrapped four times around the needle
- Two-strand couched straight stitch for the stem
- Two-strand straight stitch for the leaves and the dark lines on the petals

## CALENDULA

*Calendula officinalis*

A hero of the garden, this flower wards off pests and insects, thrives in nearly any type of soil, and is well known for its medicinal qualities. Calendula is sometimes called little calendar or little clock because it often blooms on the first of the month.

- DMC embroidery floss: 740, 741, 3362, 3854
- Four-strand satin stitch for the leaves and buds
- Four-strand straight stitch for the petals
- Two-strand couched straight stitch or two-strand backstitch for the stem

## CALIFORNIA POPPY

*Eschscholzia californica*

Poppies are one of the plant species that feature in California superblooms, a rare phenomenon in which an unusually high proportion of wildflowers blossom at the same time, creating impressively beautiful golden fields. They are also one of my favorites because they are among the first spring flowers to bloom in my garden and the very last to die in fall.

- DMC embroidery floss: 741, 900, 937, 3854
- Four-strand satin stitch for the petals
- Two-strand straight stitch for the leaves and the dark lines on the petals
- Two-strand couched straight stitch or two-strand backstitch for the stems

## CRASPEDIA

*Craspedia globosa*

Sometimes known as billy buttons or drumstick flowers, these beauties stand out with their perfectly spherical flowers, which are also wonderful dried. They are versatile for any landscape because they can be stitched as a series of French knots, or single French knots if they are closer to the horizon line.

- DMC embroidery floss: 307, 520, 728
- French knots for the flower heads, with two-strand floss wrapped two or three times around the needle; alternatively, six-strand satin stitch for flower heads when they are in the landscape background
- Six-strand couched straight stitch or six-strand backstitch for the stem

## DANDELION

*Taraxacum* species

This well-known flower is dismissed as a weed but holds so much beauty in the way that it can grow in just about any environment and under adverse conditions.

- DMC embroidery floss: 307, 613, 728, 838, 937, B5200

### Flowering Dandelion

- Two-strand straight stitch for the center of the flower
- Four-strand straight stitch for the outer petals
- Two-strand couched straight stitch or two-strand backstitch for the stem

### Seed-Head Dandelion

- Six-strand satin stitch for the center of the seed head
- Two-strand straight stitch for the inner section
- Single-strand straight stitch for the outer section

## ECHINACEA

*Echinacea* species

Also known as coneflower, echinacea's name derives from the Greek word for hedgehog, referring to the spiky seed head in the center of the flower. Indigenous people of North America discovered the medicinal properties of this plant's roots; it's now commonly used as an immune booster.

- DMC embroidery floss: 152, 838, 937, 3607, 3826
- Four-strand satin stitch for the center of the flower head
- Single-strand straight stitch for the spikes
- Four-strand long-and-short stitch for the outer petals
- Two-strand long-and-short stitch for the inner petals
- Four-strand satin stitch for the leaves
- Two-strand couched straight stitch or two-strand backstitch for the stem

## GOLDENROD

*Solidago* species

Despite its status as a weed, goldenrod benefits gardens by adding nitrogen to the soil and can be enjoyed as a tea. They can add a lovely dynamic to a foreground because of the vertical shape of the flowers.

- DMC embroidery floss: 726, 728, 937
- Two-strand couched straight stitch for the stem
- Six-strand straight stitch for the flower base
- French knots for the flower tops, with two-strand floss wrapped one or two times around the needle
- Four-strand long-and-short stitch for the leaves

## LAVENDER

*Lavandula* species

Technically, lavender is part of the mint family, though its smell is distinctively unlike other mint plants. Lavender was used in ancient Egypt and Greece for both perfume and aromatic baths, and it is still a beloved flower today because of its scent and healing power.

- DMC embroidery floss: 3042, 3052, 3740
- Two-strand couched straight stitch for the stem
- French knot for the flowers, with two-strand floss wrapped one to three times around the needle
- Four-strand straight stitch for the leaves

## MILKWEED

*Asclepias* species

Milkweed is the only plant on which monarch butterflies will lay their eggs, making it a crucial part of that beloved pollinator's life cycle. With its textured flowers and wispy seed heads, milkweed also adds a lot of visual interest to any landscape.

- DMC embroidery floss: 152, 154, 819, 3362, 3726
- Two-strand straight stitch for the large flower heads
- Two-strand couched straight stitch for the stem
- Four-strand straight stitch for the leaves
- French knots for the small flower heads, with two-strand floss wrapped one to three times around the needle

## ORIENTAL POPPY

*Papaver orientale*

These short-lived flowers bring a brilliant burst of life to the garden. They bloom for only 10 to 14 days, but their flowers are something to look forward to all year long. A popular flower for many pollinators, Oriental poppy was cultivated as long ago as 5000 BCE, and its seeds have a potent ability to relieve pain.

- DMC embroidery floss: 22, 310, 900, 937
- Four-strand straight stitch and satin stitch for the petals
- Four-strand satin stitch for the center and leaves
- Four-strand couched straight stitch or four-strand backstitch for the stems

## PRAIRIE CONEFLOWER

*Ratibida columnifera*

With their resemblance to a sombrero, these flowers are also known as Mexican hat flowers. Wonderful for gardens, they are easily grown from seed, are drought tolerant, and have an unusually long blooming season. They are similar to black-eyed Susans in color, but I choose these instead when I want downward-facing petals in my composition.

- DMC embroidery floss: 613, 726, 728, 838, 3052
- Four-strand satin stitch for the flower heads and petals
- Four-strand straight stitch for the leaves
- Two-strand couched straight stitch for the stem

## RABBITBRUSH

*Chrysothamnus* species

Rabbitbrush is the reason I fell in love with Colorado's fall landscape. These plants stay camouflaged in a muted green all summer only to blossom a brilliant yellow in fall. While other landscapes boast their fall color in the treetops, rabbitbrush transforms the ground on the plains where I live.

- DMC embroidery floss: 307, 728, 934, 937
- Four-strand straight stitch for the stems and leaves
- Six-strand straight stitch for the flower heads

## SALVIA

*Salvia* species

There are over 900 species of salvia, and they bloom in a variety of colors—blue, white, purple, pink, red, and yellow. They can create striking vertical lines in your stitched landscape. I often place them directly on the horizon line to help guide the eye up over the horizon and into the sky.

- DMC embroidery floss: 154, 327, 3042, 3362
- Six-strand straight stitch for the flowers and stems
- Single-strand straight stitch for the purple line between flower and stem

## SUNFLOWER

*Helianthus annuus*

A sunflower will follow the sun throughout the day and return to its resting point at night. After the Chernobyl and Fukushima nuclear disasters, scientists planted sunflowers because they have the remarkable ability to soak up toxins from the soil.

- DMC embroidery floss: 307, 728, 938, 988
- Six-strand satin stitch for the flower center and leaves
- Two-strand straight stitch for the petals
- Four-strand couched straight stitch for the stem

## THISTLE

*Cirsium* species

I often gripe about the thistles that take over my garden, but they win me over when they finally show their stunning, prickly flowers in late summer. Despite its beauty, thistle is indeed hard to kill and easily overwhelms other plants when it spreads. Some varieties have yellow or white flowers, but most are purple.

- DMC embroidery floss: 890, 988, 3607, 3836
- Six-strand satin stitch for the flower base
- Single-strand straight stitch for the flower base texture
- Two-strand straight stitch for the petals and leaves
- Two-strand couched straight stitch or two-strand backstitch for the stem

---

## YARROW

*Achillea millefolium*

Indigenous people of North America discovered the medicinal qualities of yarrow for easing inflammation, toothaches, headaches, and fevers. Its genus name, *Achillea*, derives from the tale of Achilles using the plant to heal a soldier's wound during the Battle of Troy. *Millefolium* translates to "thousand leaves," so named because when you look closely at its leaves, you see hundreds of smaller leaves within each section.

- DMC embroidery floss: 307, 986
- Four-strand satin stitch for the flowers
- Two-strand straight stitch for the leaves
- Two-strand couched straight stitch or two-strand backstitch for the stem

## TREE SHAPES

Sometimes you'll want the silhouette of a tree against a background of the sky. The shape will suggest either an evergreen or a deciduous tree.

### Evergreen

- DMC embroidery floss: 895
- Six-strand satin stitch

### Deciduous

- DMC embroidery floss: 895
- Six-strand satin stitch for the tree body
- Four- to six-strand straight stitch for the trunk
- Two-strand backstitch for the outline

---

## BLUE SPRUCE

*Picea pungens*

Known for its blue-green needles, this tree is perfect for adding a cooler green to the landscape. Capable of living over 600 years, the blue spruce isn't typically used as lumber because its wood is brittle, but it is a common Christmas tree.

- DMC embroidery floss: 561, 3052
- Two-strand straight stitch for the accent stitches
- Four-strand straight stitch for the base stiches

## DOUGLAS FIR

*Pseudotsuga menziesii*

Douglas fir is actually a false hemlock, not a type of fir tree, and is resistant to medium-heat wildfires. After higher intensity fires, Douglas firs can regenerate more easily than other tree species. I always think of a Douglas fir's color as being warmer than many other evergreens.

- DMC embroidery floss: 890, 3362
- Two-strand straight stitch for the accent stitches
- Four-strand straight stitch for the base stitches

## MAPLE

*Acer* species

Maples are known for their fiery autumn foliage and the sweet syrup that sugar maples produce. They have what is known as tonewood, meaning the wood itself can hold and sustain tones, so it is especially suitable for making instruments.

- DMC embroidery floss: 22, 741, 838, 900
- Four-strand satin stitch for the trunk, angling stitches as the trunk splays out
- Two-strand couched straight stitches for the branches
- Six-strand straight stitches for the leaves

## OAK

*Quercus* species

With their lobed leaves and acorn seeds, oak trees are easy to identify. There are over 400 species! Oaks have been on Earth for millennia, and trees of some species have lived up to 1,000 years.

- DMC embroidery floss: 840, 904
- Four-strand satin stitch for the trunk, angling stitches as the trunk splays out
- Two-strand couched straight stitches for the branches
- Six-strand straight stitches for the leaves

## ROCKY MOUNTAIN JUNIPER

*Juniperus scopulorum*

With their cool green foliage and bright blue berries, these trees make a great addition to any embroidered landscape. The Cheyenne and Lakota peoples both made tea from the tree to cure colds and other ailments.

- DMC embroidery floss: 319, 561, 3817
- Four-strand straight stitch for the branches
- French knots for the juniper berries, with two-strand floss wrapped one or two times around the needle

## Creating Your Own Building Block

If you want to stitch a plant that's not included as a building block, you can create your own pattern! Ideally you have a live plant to draw from. Take a cutting and put it in a vase or glass so you can observe it clearly from different angles. If you have a few flowers or specimens of the same variety, that's even better because you can more easily observe different shapes and angles.

If you don't have a live plant, look up botanical illustrations and photos. Use a sketchbook to record your observations, but be respectful of other artists' work and don't directly copy an illustration.

Observe and sketch the following:

- The angle of the stem
- The leaf shape
- How many petals are on each flower
- Whether the petals are flat or pointed at the end
- What the flower looks like before it blooms
- What the flower looks like from the side
- What the flower looks like from above

### SCALE THE DRAWING

Think about how big the plant will be in your final piece, and draw a few angles of it at that scale. I generally have three or four different angles of a flower when I'm stitching them in a field. Trace your drawing in a heavy black marker, and you're ready to transfer it to fabric.

### CHOOSE THE THREAD COLORS

If you don't have a live plant, look at photos or botanical illustrations. I prefer studying botanical illustrations for their closely observed details, but be aware that such illustrations often have inaccurate color. When you'd like the plant to have a lot of detail—if a flower is in the foreground of a large hoop, for example—make sure to choose a light, midtone, and dark version of its petal color and foliage.

### CHOOSE THE STITCHES

Decide what kind of stitch will best capture the different parts of your plant. For flowers, I generally use straight stitch or satin stitch for petals, French knots or satin stitch for the center, backstitch or straight stitch for the stem, and satin stitch for leaves.

### TIPS FOR STITCHING FLOWER PETALS

I have some tried-and-true techniques to share:

- Begin in the back. Start with the petals that other petals will overlap.
- When stitching an elongated petal, disregard the usual satin-stitch rule of working across the shortest length, which would make the petal look unnatural. Stitch in the same direction that the plant grows.

For petals with pointed tips:

- Begin the stitches along a line at the wide base of the petal, but end at a single point about one tenth of the total length from the tip of the petal.
- To create the pointed tip, bring the needle up at the tip and push it back down just shy of the base. Repeat once or twice, until the point smoothly blends into the rest of the petal.

Use thread to create a variety of petal shapes, layering in color to add dimension.

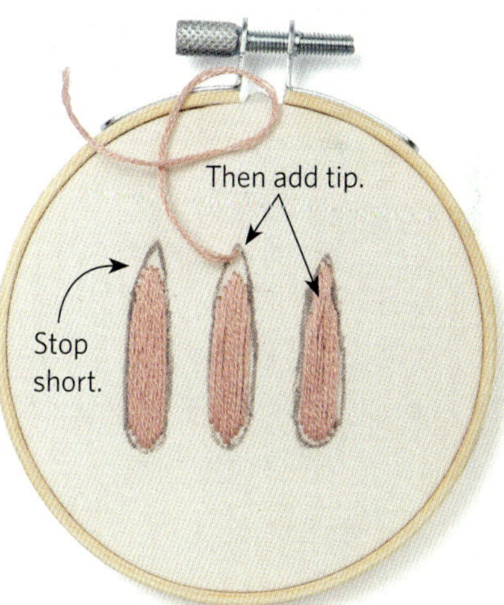

## BIG BLUESTEM

*Andropogon gerardii*

In summer this grass is blue-green. In fall it turns a brilliant brownish red, making it a versatile addition for landscapes.

- DMC embroidery floss: 163, 520
- Two-strand straight stitch for the blades
- Two-strand couched straight stitch for the accent blades in front

## BLUE FESCUE

*Festuca ovina* 'Glauca'

As its common name suggests, this grass is blue-green, so I often use it when I want a cooler color in my landscape. Blue fescue is very stiff, standing out easily in a landscape with its incredibly straight blades that angle out from a central root system. Tan stalks with seed heads shoot out of the central clump of grass when the plant is in bloom.

- DMC embroidery floss: 163, 319, 422
- Two-strand straight stitch for the blades of grass
- Single-strand straight stitch for the tips of seed heads

## BLUE GRAMA

*Bouteloua gracilis*

This is one of my favorite grasses to stitch because of its bright green stalks and unique, angled seed heads. Blue grama is native to North America and thrives in dry regions since it's drought resistant.

- DMC embroidery floss: 422, 890, 989
- Two-strand straight stitch for the blades and seed heads
- Single-strand straight stitch for the tips of seed heads

## SWITCHGRASS

*Panicum virgatum*

Switchgrass changes color throughout the seasons, making it perfect for summer, fall, and winter landscapes. It has purplish-red seed heads in midsummer and turns a deep yellow in fall.

- DMC embroidery floss: 520, 739, 840, 3053
- Two-strand straight stitch for the base of the blades
- Single-strand straight stitch for the top of the blades

## BEET

*Beta vulgaris*

These deep red root vegetables can also be a rich golden color. The entire plant is edible, from the leaves to the root. When I add them to a landscape, I often put them at the bottom of my middle ground so they appear to be underground, with their roots visible.

- DMC embroidery floss: 819, 890, 3857
- Four-strand satin stitch for the root
- Two-strand straight stitch for the stems and leaves
- Single-strand straight stitch for the root texture

## CARROT

*Daucus carota*

Carrots can come in just about any color: yellow, orange, red, purple, white, even black! I treat them similarly to beets in a landscape, placing them in front of my middle ground, revealing the roots.

- DMC embroidery floss: 22, 154, 520, 739, 741, 988, 3053
- Four-strand satin stitch for the root
- Two-strand straight stitch for the stems and leaves
- Single-strand straight stitch for the root texture

## PUMPKIN

*Cucurbita* species

Part of the gourd family, pumpkins ripen and mature in fall. They originated in Central America and are now grown on every continent except Antarctica.

- DMC embroidery floss: 741, 838, 895, 900, 988
- Six-strand satin stitch for the pumpkin and leaves
- Two-strand couched straight stitch for the stems and tendrils
- Single-strand couched straight stitch for the pumpkin texture

## TOMATO

*Solanum lycopersicum*

The common name of this garden favorite comes from the Aztec word *tomatl*, meaning "plump fruit." Though famous for their frequent red color, tomatoes may have originally been golden. Humans have bred over 10,000 varieties!

- DMC embroidery floss: 22, 666, 987
- Two-strand couched straight stitch for the stem
- Two-strand straight stitch for the leaves
- French knots for the fruit, with two-strand floss wrapped two or three times around the needle

## DRIED BIG BLUESTEM

Big bluestem captures my attention in fall when it turns brownish red. I typically add this to my embroidered landscapes when I want to create a dark area in the composition.

- DMC embroidery floss: 838, 975
- Two-strand straight stitch for the blades
- Single-strand straight stitch for the seed heads

## DEAD RABBITBRUSH

Rabbitbrush is at its most beautiful when yellow in fall, but it still adds interest to any landscape because of the cloudlike, light-colored seed heads that sit atop the shrub.

- DMC embroidery floss: 422, 612, 613, 782, 838
- Two-strand straight stitch for the stem
- Six-strand straight stitch for the flower heads
- French knot for the seed heads, with two-strand floss wrapped two times around the needle
- Two-strand couched straight stitch for the bent grass in front

## DRIED FLAX

Flax seed heads are tiny balls sitting on the delicate wisps of the stems. I use these to add whimsical pops of light brown French knots in my landscapes.

- DMC embroidery floss: 422, 612, 829
- Two-strand couched straight stitch for the stem
- French knot for the seed head, with two-strand floss wrapped three or four times around the needle

## DRIED SWITCHGRASS

When switchgrass begins to die, it develops tiny, beautiful, light brown seed heads that stand out against the darker brown of the grass's stalk. It is perfect for adding subtle details to a landscape.

- DMC embroidery floss: 680, 739, 838
- Two-strand straight stitch for the blade
- French knot for the seed head, with two-strand floss wrapped one time around the needle

## SUNFLOWER SEED HEADS

Every winter I am drawn to the stark dark brown, almost black sunflower seed heads that dot the landscape. They are so dark, they can seem unreal. I often stitch them in a dark brown (as seen here), but I sometimes opt for black to really make them pop (see An Ode to Dead Grass, page 161).

- DMC embroidery floss: 612, 838, 840
- Two-strand couched straight stitch for the stem and petals
- Four-strand satin stitch for the seed head; alternatively, French knot for the seed head, with two-strand floss wrapped three or four times around the needle

---

## ECHINACEA SEED HEADS

Echinacea (or coneflower) seed heads are similar visually to sunflower seed heads, but their petals point downward, and their stems are more reddish brown.

- DMC embroidery floss: 613, 838, 975
- Two-strand couched straight stitch for the stem
- Two-strand straight stitch for the dead petals
- Four-strand satin stitch for the seed head; alternatively, French knot for the seed head, with two-strand floss wrapped three or four times around the needle

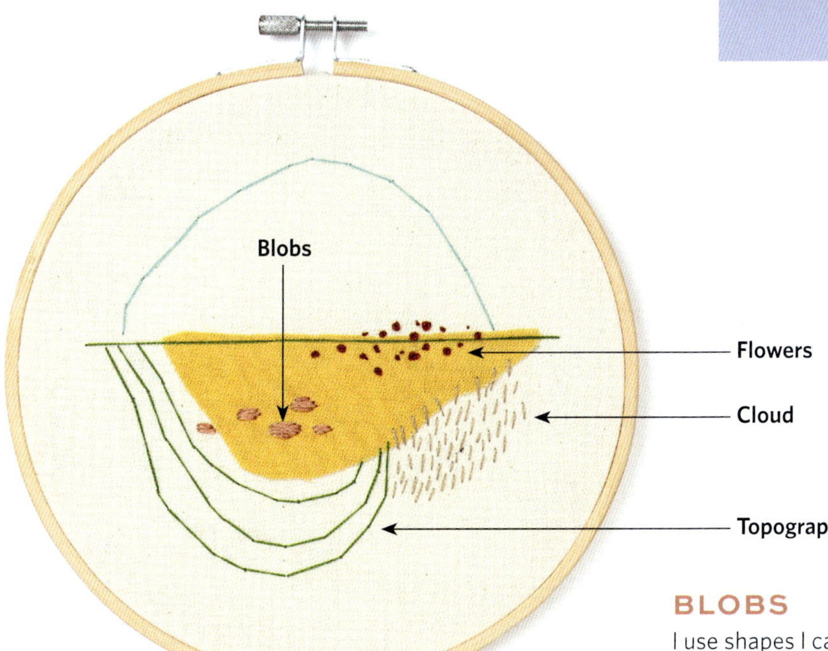


## BLOBS

I use shapes I call blobs purely as a compositional tool in my landscapes. They don't necessarily represent anything, but they playfully help lead the eye around the landscape.

- Six-strand satin stitch in any suitable color

## FLOWERS

Sometimes I need a pop of color in my composition and don't want to base my stitching on a specific plant. In these instances, I add French knots or a couple of satin stitches in the color I need and let them read as flowers in the landscape.

### French knot version

- French knots in any suitable color, with two- to six-strand floss wrapped one to four times around the needle

### Satin-stitch version

- Six-strand satin stitch in any suitable color

## CLOUD

I use this term to refer to scattered gatherings of stitches that create "clouds" of color in a landscape. This abstract element functions a lot like adding watercolor under a middle ground, but instead it's a series of small straight stitches.

- Two-strand straight stitch in any cloud color

## TOPOGRAPHICAL DETAIL

This is another way to extend the middle ground. I often use it as a playful nod to topographical maps.

- Two-strand couched straight stitch or backstitch in any suitable color

CHAPTER 7

# BUILDING-BLOCK PROJECTS

Let's look at how the building blocks of a landscape can come together into finished compositions. Feel free to swap out plants, colors, and backgrounds in any of these patterns for a customized piece. I hope that once you complete a few of the projects, you'll be energized to use the compositional ideas and techniques you've practiced to create an embroidered landscape inspired by your own surroundings.

# CHOOSE YOUR CHALLENGE

I've designed these patterns with varying levels of complexity.

**ONE NEEDLE.** Projects with an icon of a single needle use mostly essential embroidery techniques (see Chapter 3) and up to one experimental technique (see Chapter 4). The compositions and layering of materials are simple and straightforward.

**TWO NEEDLES.** Projects with an icon of two needles include more steps and use up to three experimental techniques in a single piece. The layering of techniques gets slightly more complicated.

**THREE NEEDLES.** Projects with an icon of three needles use every experimental technique we have in our toolbox. The base layer of stitching will be dense enough that you need to use observation instead of pattern tracing to place some of the foreground details.

## Using Building-Block Patterns

The patterns on the following pages all draw inspiration from the building blocks we explored in the previous chapter. The directions for these projects sometimes differ from those in the building-block sections, depending on how the landscape is structured, so always follow the written directions for each pattern. However, referring back to the building-block sections will allow you to see how a landscape can be built using simple compositional elements and empower you to create unique landscapes of your own.

# MEMORY: A MENTAL MAP

With this imaginary landscape, I wanted to capture the patchwork quality that fields of grass often have. Satin stitching the middle ground without much foreground detail on top accentuates and maintains the patchwork look. The middle ground anchors the composition, while the straight-stitched "blobs" and the red French knot flowers move our eye around the piece. The concentric lines at the bottom of the middle ground echo topographical maps, nodding to the concept that the landscape is a mental map of a field rather than an actual observed field.

## BUILDING BLOCKS

Basic Grass Field, page 116

Cloud, page 143

Tree Shapes, pages 131–133

Abstract Flowers, page 143

Blobs, page 143

## COLOR AND STITCH GUIDE

| CODE LETTER | STITCHES |
|---|---|
| **A** | Satin stitch |
| **B** | Straight stitch |
| **C** | Couched straight stitch |
| **D** | French knot |

| CODE NUMBER | DMC EMBROIDERY FLOSS COLOR # |
|---|---|
| **1** | 935 |
| **2** | 3347 |
| **3** | 904 |
| **4** | 733 |
| **5** | 307 |
| **6** | 3726 |
| **7** | 900 |
| **8** | 3064 |

### OTHER MATERIALS

- Basic supplies (see Chapter 2), including a 10" embroidery hoop and two layers of Kona cotton quilting fabric (in natural), cut into a 14" circle

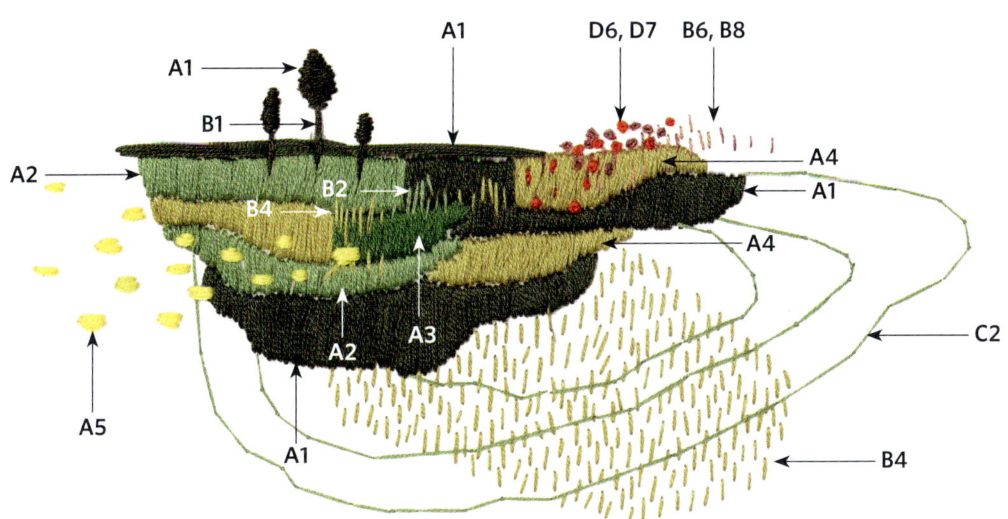

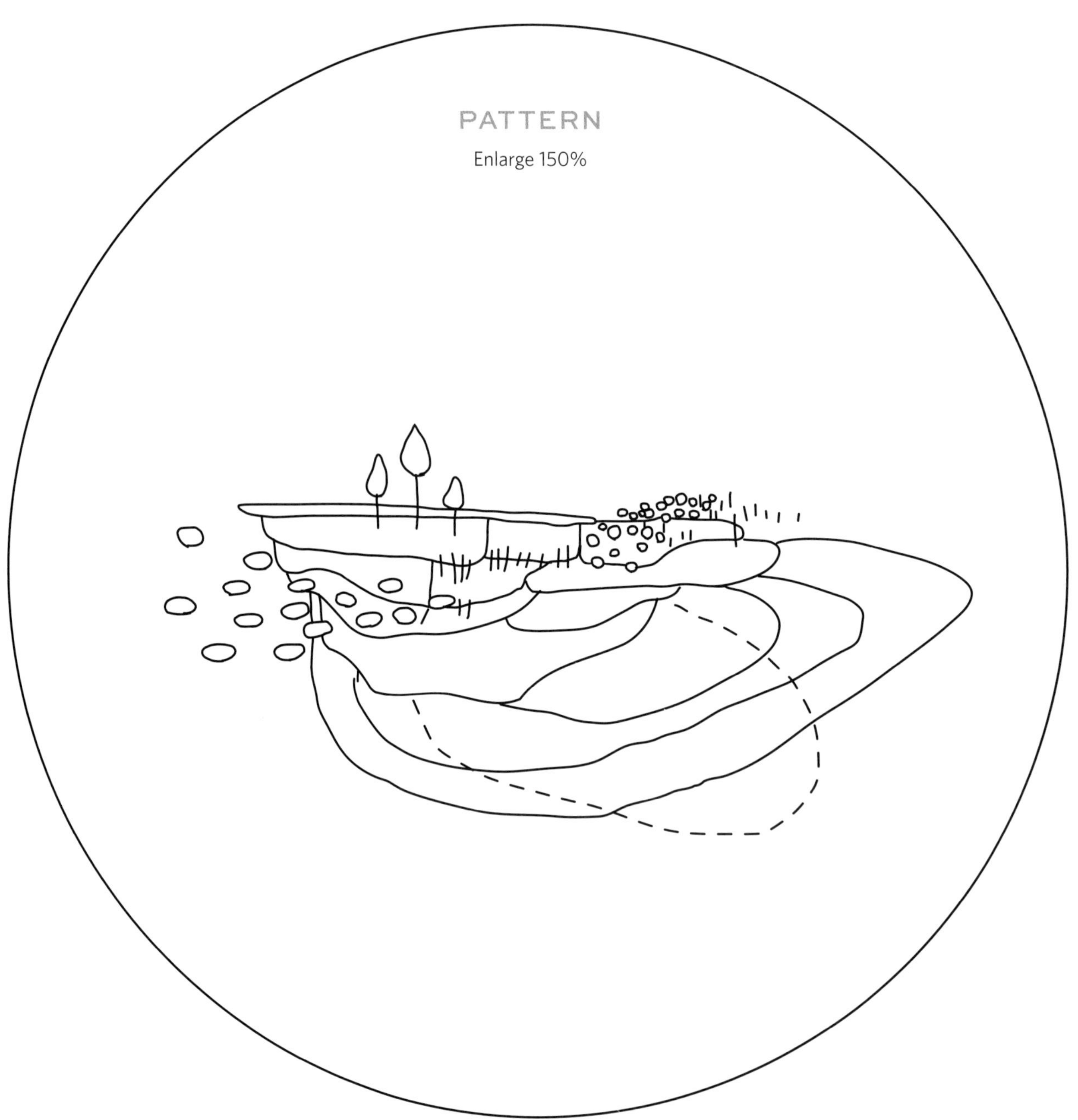
PATTERN
Enlarge 150%

## Transfer the Pattern

Using a water-soluble fabric marker, transfer the pattern onto the cloth. For the cloud of small vertical straight stitches at the bottom of the piece, I recommend outlining the shape of the entire cloud, not each individual straight stitch.

## Stitch the Middle Ground

Use a six-strand satin stitch to fill the patchwork area with colors 935, 3347, 904, and 733.

Add horizontal six-strand satin stitches in color 935 at the top of the middle ground to emphasize the horizon line.

Add the topographical map lines with a two-strand couched straight stitch in color 3347.

## Stitch the Background

Using color 935, stitch the tops of the trees with a horizontal four-strand satin stitch, then use a six-strand straight stitch to create the trunks.

## Stitch the Foreground

Use a six-strand satin stitch to create the yellow blobs in color 307. Each blob needs only two stitches side by side.

Use two-strand French knots—wrapped two or three times around the needle—for the flowers near the horizon line in colors 3726 and 900. You want a variety of purple and red, with the red advancing farther down the field than the purple.

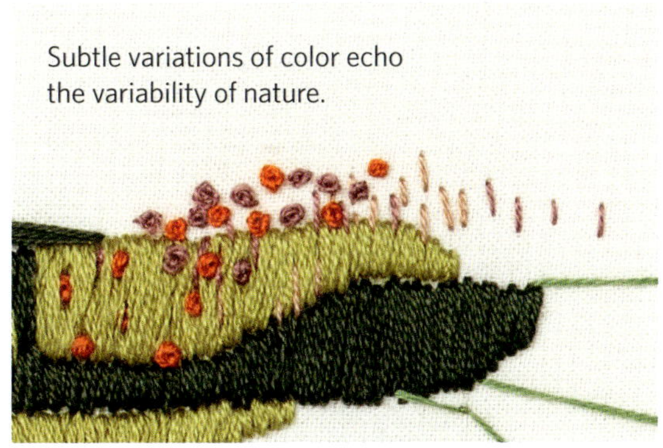

Subtle variations of color echo the variability of nature.

After the knots, use two-strand floss in colors 3726 and 3064 for a few vertical straight stitches along the horizon line.

Add a line of grass with two-strand vertical straight stitches in the middle of the patchwork middle ground in colors 3347 and 733.

Use ¼"–½" two-strand straight stitches to create the cloud in color 733. Fill the edges first before moving into the center. Keep the length, distance, and spacing a little inconsistent.

## Finish the Hoop

Run your entire hoop under hot water to wash out the pattern transfer marks and tighten your fabric. Refer to Finishing Your Embroidery (page 56).

# SUPERBLOOM

The superblooms of California poppies inspired this hoop. A superbloom occurs when dormant wildflower seeds in the soil all blossom at the same time—a rare phenomenon that happens only when the exact right amount of rain falls within a certain time frame under certain conditions. If there is too much moisture, invasive grasses grow first and crowd out the wildflowers. The flowers need enough heat to germinate, but too much will kill them.

A satin-stitched middle ground creates a canvas for the California poppies. The flowers are a combination of French knots and straight stitches because variation always makes a landscape look more natural.

## BUILDING BLOCKS

Outlined Sky, pages 120–121

California Poppies, pages 124–125

Abstract Flowers, page 143

## COLOR AND STITCH GUIDE

| CODE LETTER | STITCHES |
|---|---|
| **A** | Satin stitch |
| **B** | Straight stitch |
| **C** | Couched straight stitch |
| **D** | French knot |
| **E** | Backstitch |

| CODE NUMBER | DMC EMBROIDERY FLOSS COLOR # |
|---|---|
| **1** | 319 |
| **2** | 987 |
| **3** | 561 |
| **4** | 3362 |
| **5** | 3053 |
| **6** | 741 |
| **7** | 740 |

### OTHER MATERIALS

- Basic supplies (see Chapter 2), including an 8" embroidery hoop and two layers of Kona cotton quilting fabric (in natural), cut into a 12" circle

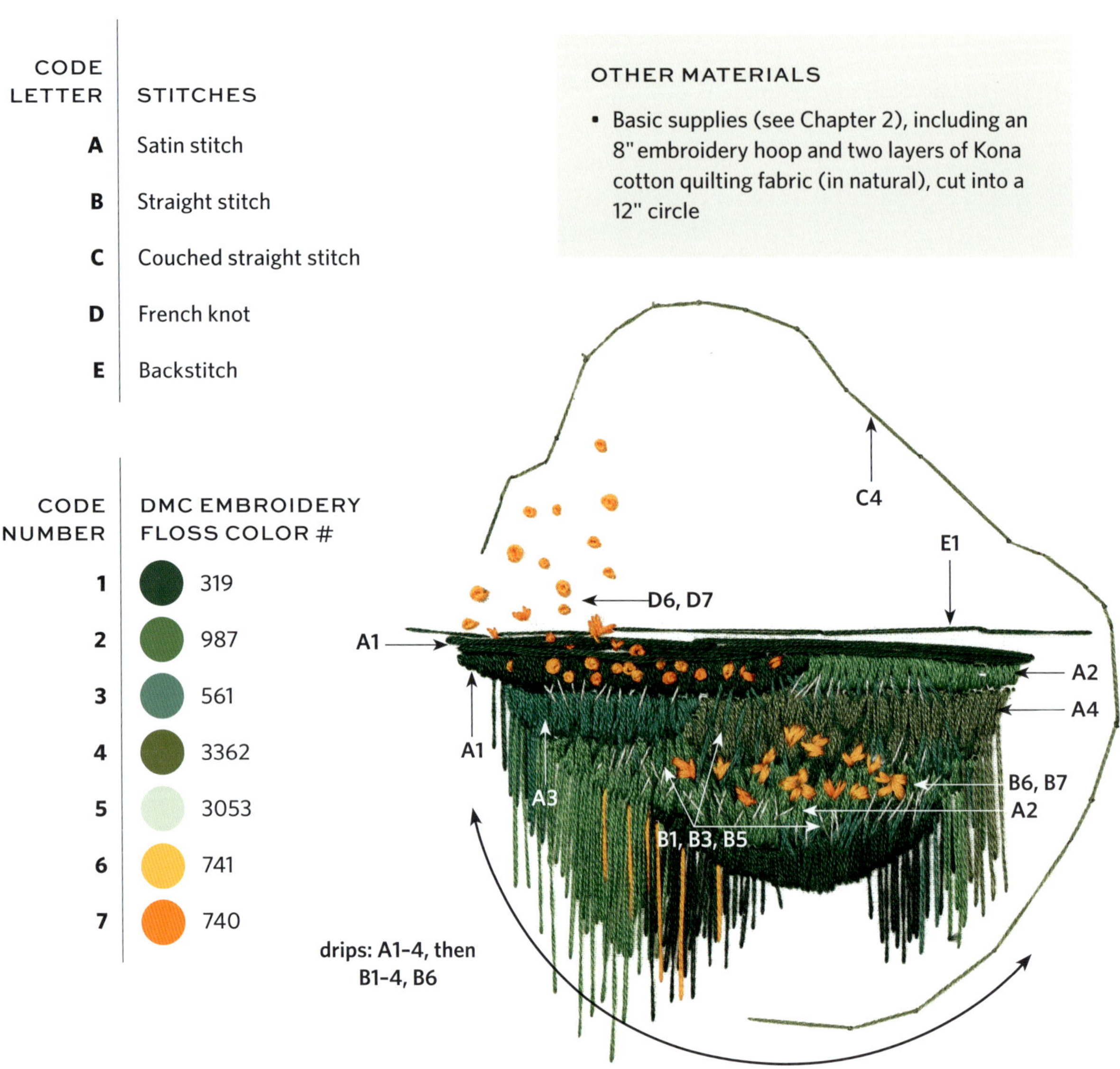

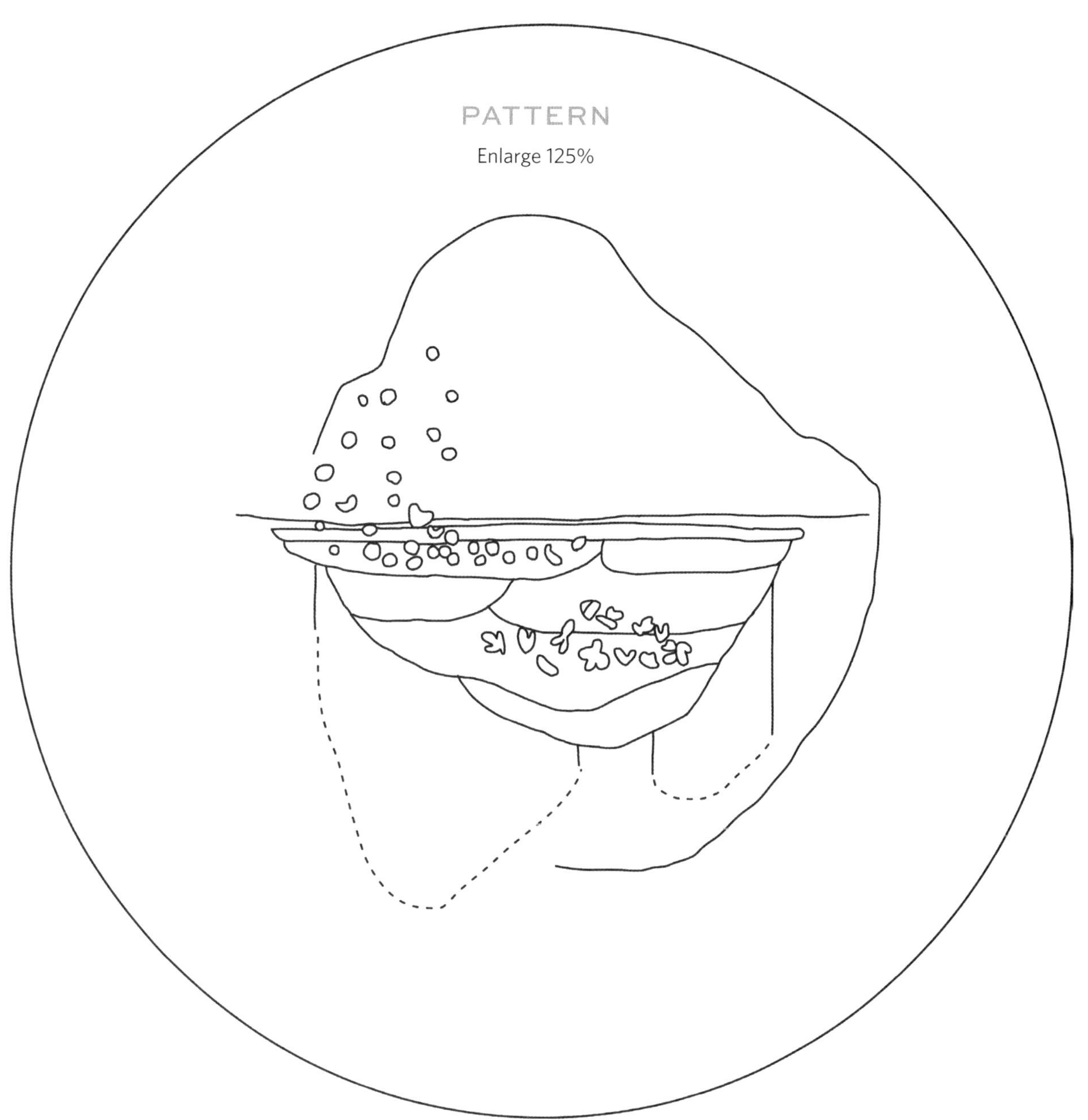
PATTERN
Enlarge 125%

## Transfer the Pattern

Using a water-soluble fabric marker, transfer the pattern onto the cloth.

## Stitch the Middle Ground

Use vertical six-strand satin stitches to fill the middle ground. Begin closest to the horizon line and work your way down. Use colors 319, 987, 561, and 3362.

Add horizontal six-strand satin stitches at the top of the middle ground in color 319 to emphasize the horizon line.

Add some vertical two-strand straight stitches in colors 319 and 561 to blend the patchwork together and create a grasslike effect. Next add more vertical straight stitches with a single strand of floss in 3053.

Add drips with a six-strand satin stitch in colors 319, 987, 561, and 3362, matching each color with the satin-stitched section it extends from. End the bottom of each stitch at different points for the driplike effect. Once you have a solid satin-stitched base built below the middle ground, switch to two-strand floss and extend the drip line with stitches that are approximately 2" long and spaced about ¼" apart. Making some of the drips orange color 741 lends pops of vibrancy.

## Stitch the Background

Create the sky outline in color 3362 with a two-strand couched straight stitch, extending the line below the middle ground in an arc.

Use a two-strand backstitch to create a horizon line that sits just above the middle ground in color 319.

## Stitch the Foreground

You won't be able to see pattern markings on top of the middle ground thread, so refer to the color guide for placement of the flowers.

Stitch about 10 poppies in the bottom of the field with four-strand straight stitches in colors 741 and 740. Each flower is minimally sketched with three to five petals. Alternate colors for variation.

Continuing to vary the colors of the poppies, stitch a series of French knots on the left side of the composition using four-strand floss wrapped one or two times around the needle. Each flower is composed of a cluster of one to three French knots.

## Finish the Hoop

Run your entire hoop under hot water to wash out the pattern transfer marks and tighten your fabric. Refer to Finishing Your Embroidery (page 56).

# HEALING FLOWERS

If you are in a season of hardship right now or have a friend in need, this hoop design could be an opportunity to thoughtfully focus on healing. I stitched craspedia, lavender, and goldenrod, respectively associated with health, serenity, and wholeness. See page 117 for the meanings of other plants and choose what speaks to you. I used wool roving for the middle ground, but you could use watercolor for a different look.

## BUILDING BLOCKS

Patchwork Grass Field, pages 118–119

Craspedia, pages 124–125

Goldenrod, pages 126–127

Lavender, pages 126–127

## COLOR AND STITCH GUIDE

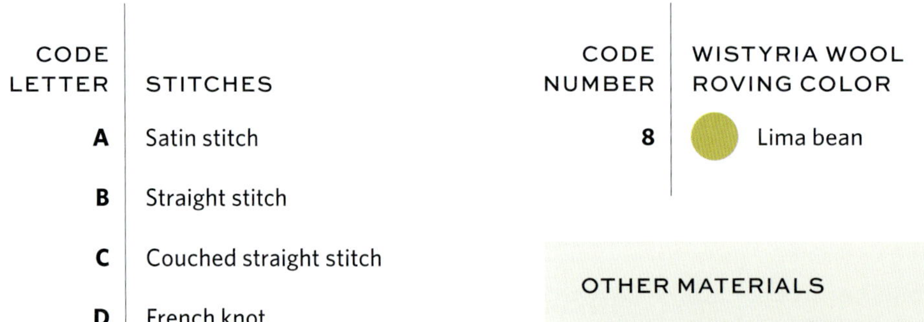

| CODE LETTER | STITCHES |
|---|---|
| **A** | Satin stitch |
| **B** | Straight stitch |
| **C** | Couched straight stitch |
| **D** | French knot |

| CODE NUMBER | WISTYRIA WOOL ROVING COLOR |
|---|---|
| **8** | Lima bean |

### OTHER MATERIALS

- Basic supplies (see Chapter 2), including a 6" embroidery hoop and two layers of Kona cotton quilting fabric (in natural), cut into a 10" circle

| CODE NUMBER | DMC EMBROIDERY FLOSS COLOR # |
|---|---|
| **1** | 3362 |
| **2** | 935 |
| **3** | 372 |
| **4** | 728 |
| **5** | 3042 |
| **6** | 3740 |
| **7** | 307 |

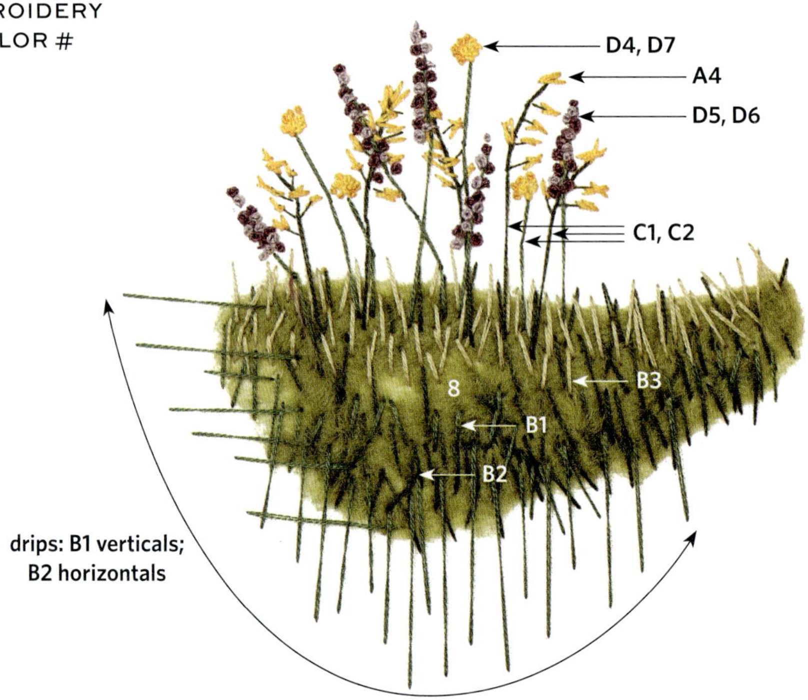

D4, D7
A4
D5, D6
C1, C2
B3
8
B1
B2
**drips: B1 verticals; B2 horizontals**

## PATTERN

Copy at 100%

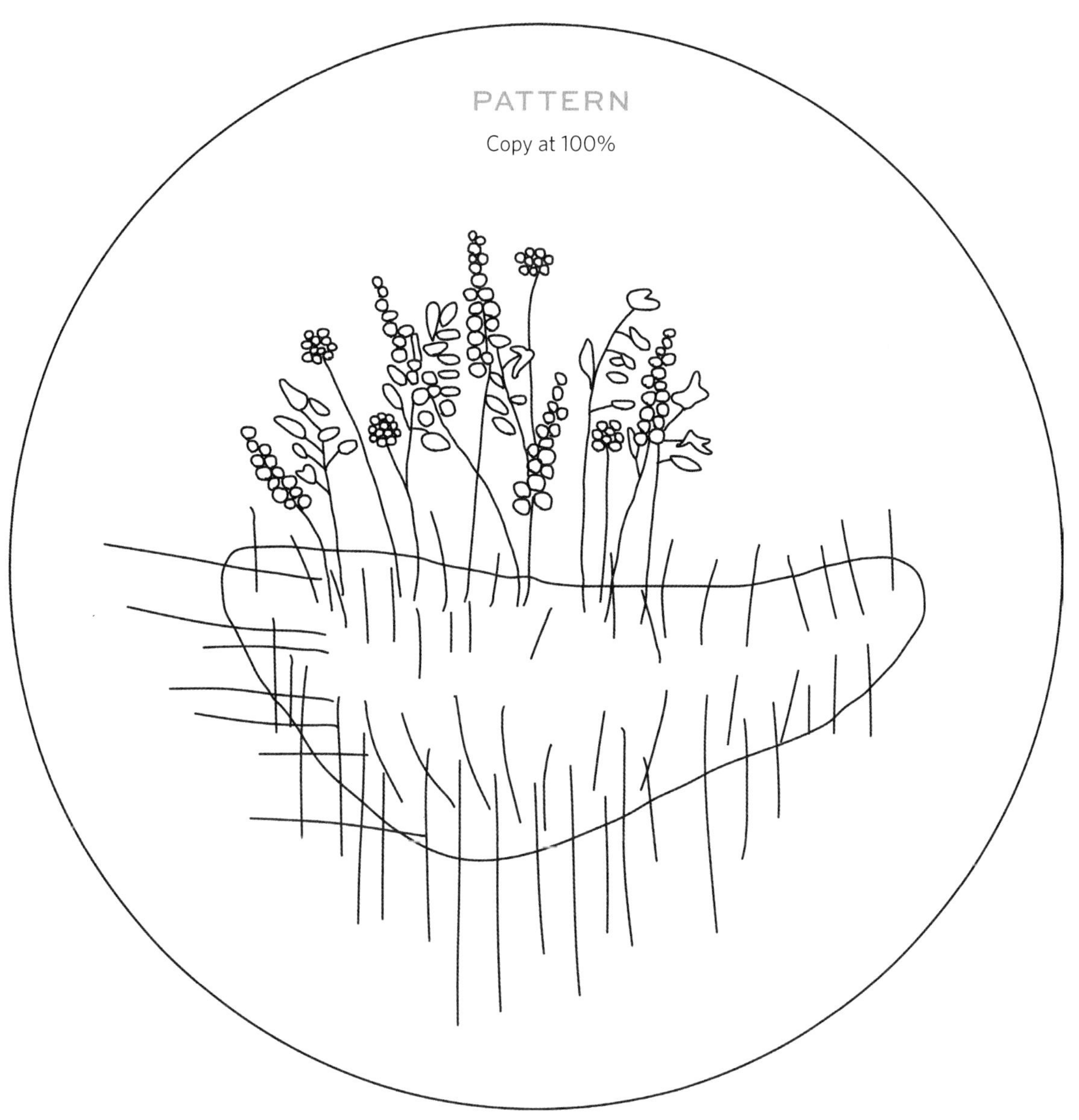

## Transfer the Pattern

Using a water-soluble fabric marker, transfer the pattern onto the cloth.

## Stitch the Middle Ground

Lay down some lima bean–colored wool roving. Always use a little more than you think you need. Anchor the roving with 10 two-strand straight stitches in color 3362, spacing them across the middle of the wool.

Begin stitching layers of grass, creating a gradient with the darkest dark at the bottom in color 935, then color 3362 for the midtone in the middle, and ending with the lightest light at the top in color 372. Each grass blade is a two-strand straight stitch about ½" long.

For the drips, use two-strand straight stitches in both horizontal and vertical lines. Use color 3362 for the vertical stitches and 935 for the horizontal. Vary the length.

## Stitch the Foreground

It's time to heal with flowers!

**GOLDENROD:** Use a two-strand couched straight stitch in color 935 for each plant stem. Use a single-strand straight stitch in the same color to create the flower stalks coming off the main stem. Create the flower with a two-strand satin stitch in color 728.

**LAVENDER:** Use a two-strand couched straight stitch for each stem, varying between colors 3362 and 935. Create the flowers with small French knots, wrapping two strands of floss one or two times around the needle, varying between colors 3042 and 3740.

**CRASPEDIA:** Use a two-strand couched straight stitch for each stem, varying between colors 3362 and 935. Create the ball of each flower with clusters of two-strand French knots wrapped one to three times around the needle. Use color 307 on the right side of each ball and color 728 on the left to create a gradient.

## Finish the Hoop

Run your entire hoop under hot water to wash out the pattern transfer marks and tighten your fabric. Refer to Finishing Your Embroidery (page 56).

# AN ODE TO DEAD GRASS

I used to hate winter in Colorado. I grew up in upstate New York with expectations that the ground becomes white in winter. The snow on the northern plains of Colorado is infrequent and usually melts within a week, leaving unsightly brown patches of dead grass. Slowly but surely I began to fall in love with the dead grass: its texture, its shadows, its wistful wispiness. One of the most beautiful moments of a winter on the plains is when the dark brown—almost black—seed heads of summer's flowers stand out against the bright, nearly white grass. I hoped to capture that moment in this hoop.

## BUILDING BLOCKS

Wet-Painted Sky, pages 120-121

Sunflower Seed Heads, page 142

## COLOR AND STITCH GUIDE

| CODE LETTER | STITCHES |
|---|---|
| **A** | Satin stitch |
| **B** | Straight stitch |
| **C** | Couched straight stitch |

| CODE NUMBER | WISTYRIA WOOL ROVING COLOR |
|---|---|
| **6** | Medium gray |

| CODE NUMBER | MARIE'S WATERCOLOR PAINTS |
|---|---|
| **7** | Prussian blue + White + Raw umber |

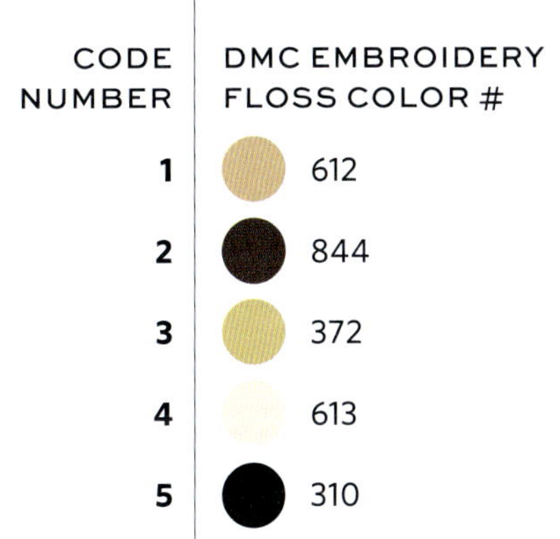

| CODE NUMBER | DMC EMBROIDERY FLOSS COLOR # |
|---|---|
| **1** | 612 |
| **2** | 844 |
| **3** | 372 |
| **4** | 613 |
| **5** | 310 |

## OTHER MATERIALS

- Basic supplies (see Chapter 2), including a 6" embroidery hoop and two layers of Kona cotton quilting fabric (in natural), cut into a 10" circle
- Paintbrush

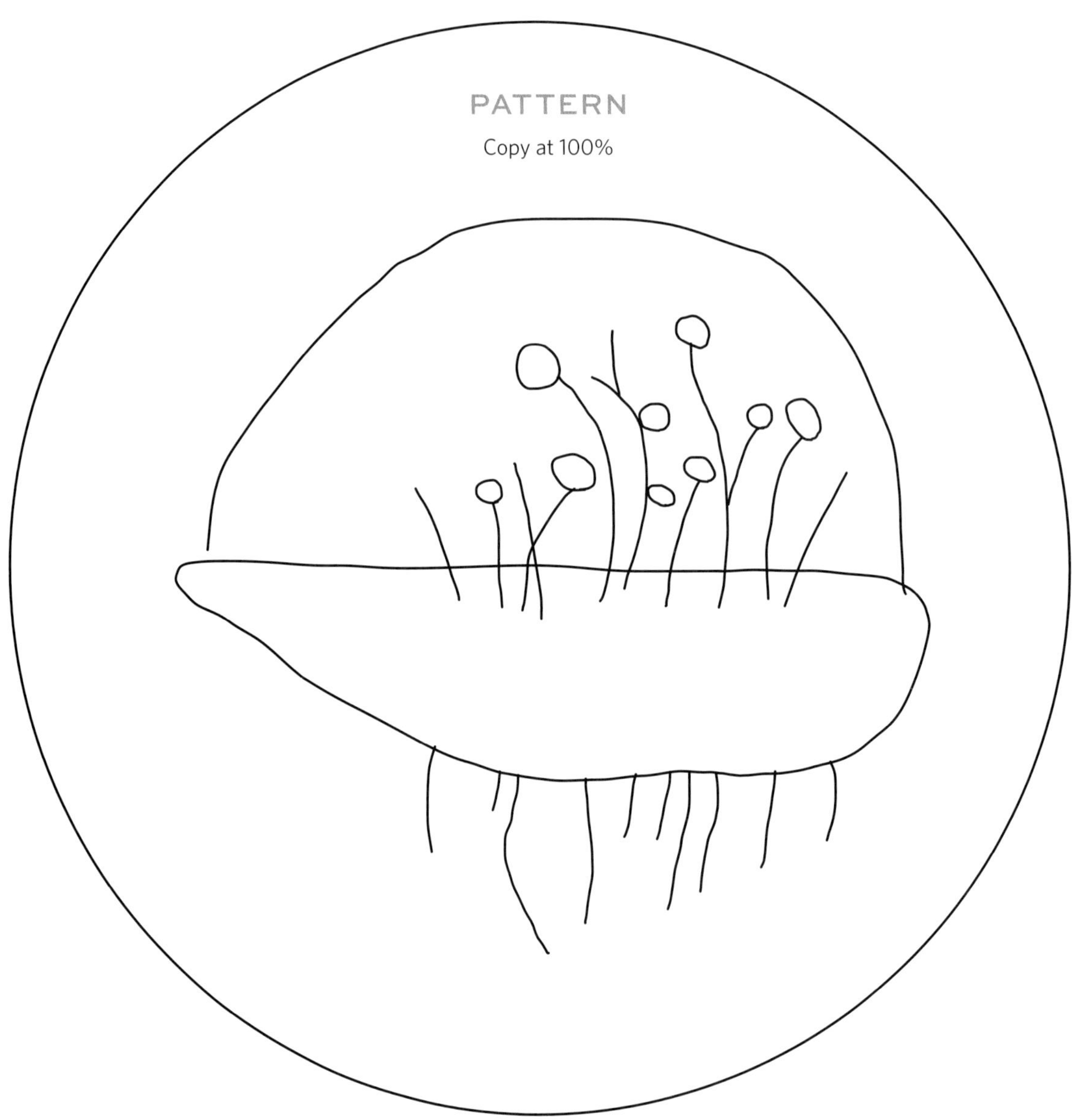
PATTERN
Copy at 100%

## Prepare the Hoop

Run the hoop and fabric under hot water to tighten and smooth your fabric. Let it dry completely.

## Paint the Watercolor

Make sure you practice on scrap fabric before you apply paint to your final piece! Mix five parts Prussian blue with one part white. Add a dot of raw umber to mute the color.

Wet the fabric with a paintbrush and clean water in a semicircle shape, starting at the horizon line and ending about 2" from the edge of the hoop. Marking the horizon line with a heat-erasable pen before you paint might help.

Soak the brush with water and pick up some paint. Apply paint at the horizon line, letting it bleed across the wet area and a bit beyond. Let the fabric dry before moving on.

## Transfer the Pattern

Using a heat-erasable pen, transfer the pattern onto the cloth.

## Stitch the Middle Ground

Lay down the wool roving. Always use a little more than you think you need. Anchor the roving with 10 two-strand straight stitches spaced along the entirety of the wool in color 612.

Start with the darkest dark in color 844 as the base layer of grass. Use ½" two-strand straight stitches to scatter grass blades over the entire piece of wool.

Add ½" two-strand straight stitches in color 612, then switch to single-strand straight stitches in colors 372 and 612. The goal is to create a gradient in the middle ground from dark to light, so stop short of the bottom area.

Use ½" single-strand straight stitches in the lightest light color (613) over the top half of the middle ground.

## Stitch the Foreground

Create a drip effect that suggests plant roots with two-strand straight stitches that extend about 1½" below the wool in color 844. Use a couched straight stitch to curve some of the drips.

Use six-strand satin stitches in color 310 to add black seed heads in the sky. Add dead petals with single strand couched straight stitch. Create each stem with single-strand couched straight stitches connected to the seed head.

## Finish the Hoop

Use a hair dryer to remove any residual markings. Refer to Finishing Your Embroidery (page 56).

# EVERGREEN

When I set out to design this hoop, I wanted small evergreen trees to dot the landscape and create the main movement in the composition. I used the scale of the trees to create perspective, with the largest trees in the foreground, stitching them smaller as they recede into the background.

## BUILDING BLOCKS

Patchwork Grass Field, pages 118–119

Fabric-Collage Sky, pages 120–121

Outlined Mountains, pages 120–121

Douglas Fir, pages 132–133

## COLOR AND STITCH GUIDE

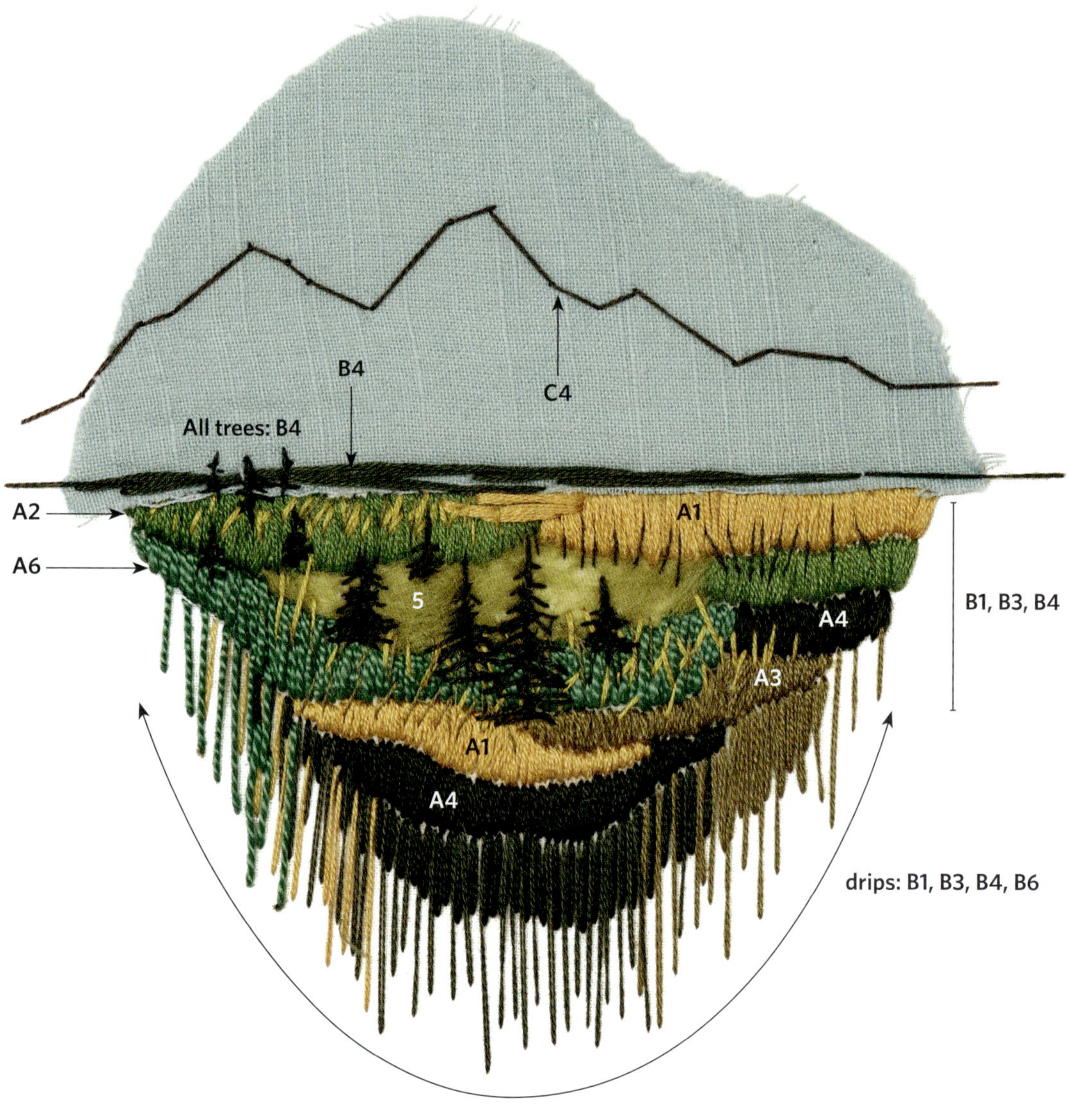

| CODE LETTER | STITCHES |
|---|---|
| A | Satin stitch |
| B | Straight stitch |
| C | Couched straight stitch |

| CODE NUMBER | DMC EMBROIDERY FLOSS COLOR # |
|---|---|
| 1 | 833 |
| 2 | 937 |
| 3 | 3011 |
| 4 | 934 |

| CODE NUMBER | WISTYRIA WOOL ROVING COLOR |
|---|---|
| 5 | Lima bean |

| CODE NUMBER | DMC PEARL COTTON EMBROIDERY THREAD (SIZE 5) |
|---|---|
| 6 | 501 |

### OTHER MATERIALS

- Basic supplies (see Chapter 2), including an 8" embroidery hoop and two layers of Kona cotton quilting fabric (in natural), cut into a 12" circle
- Blue fabric (for the sky; see page 24)

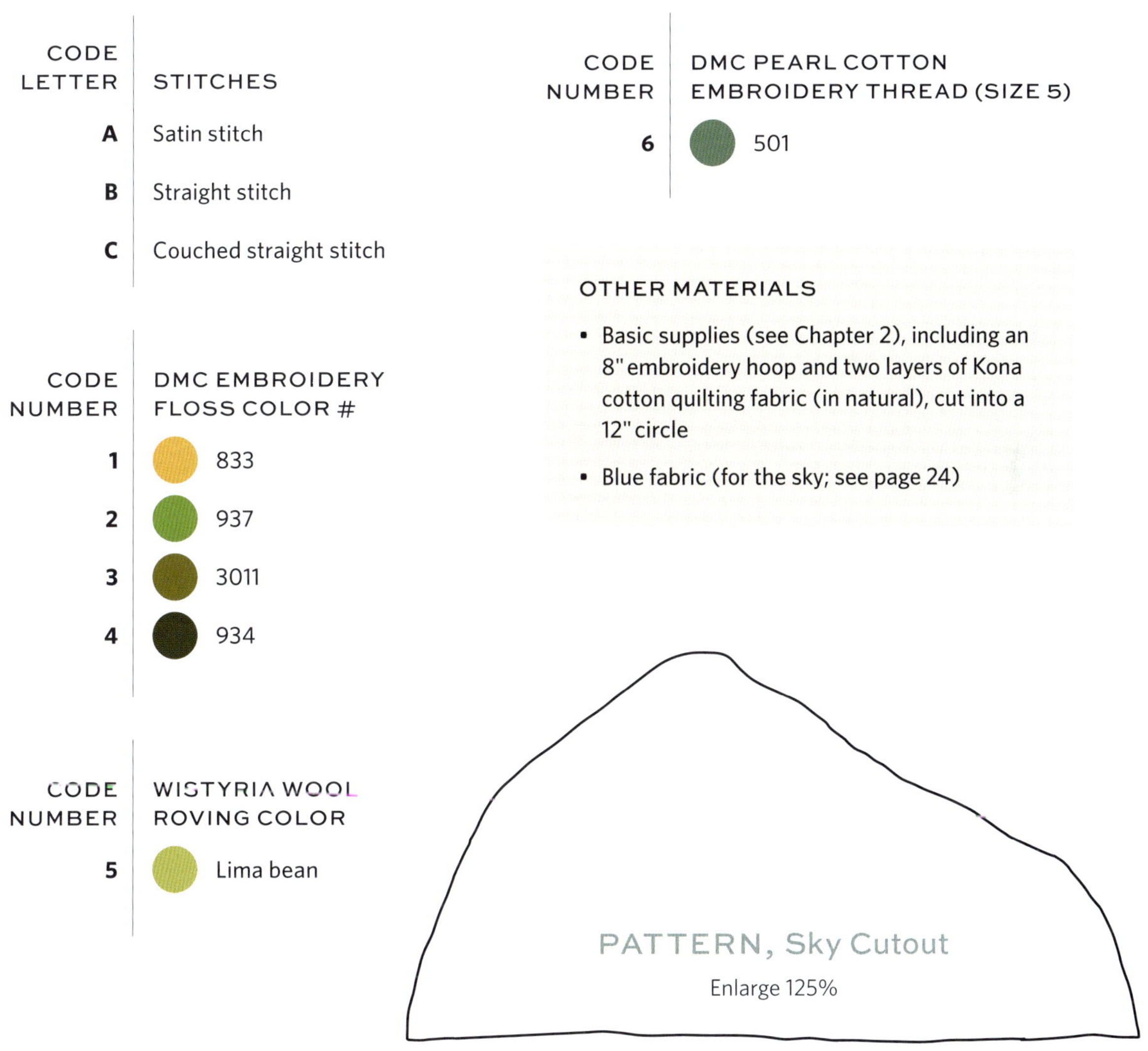

PATTERN, Sky Cutout

Enlarge 125%

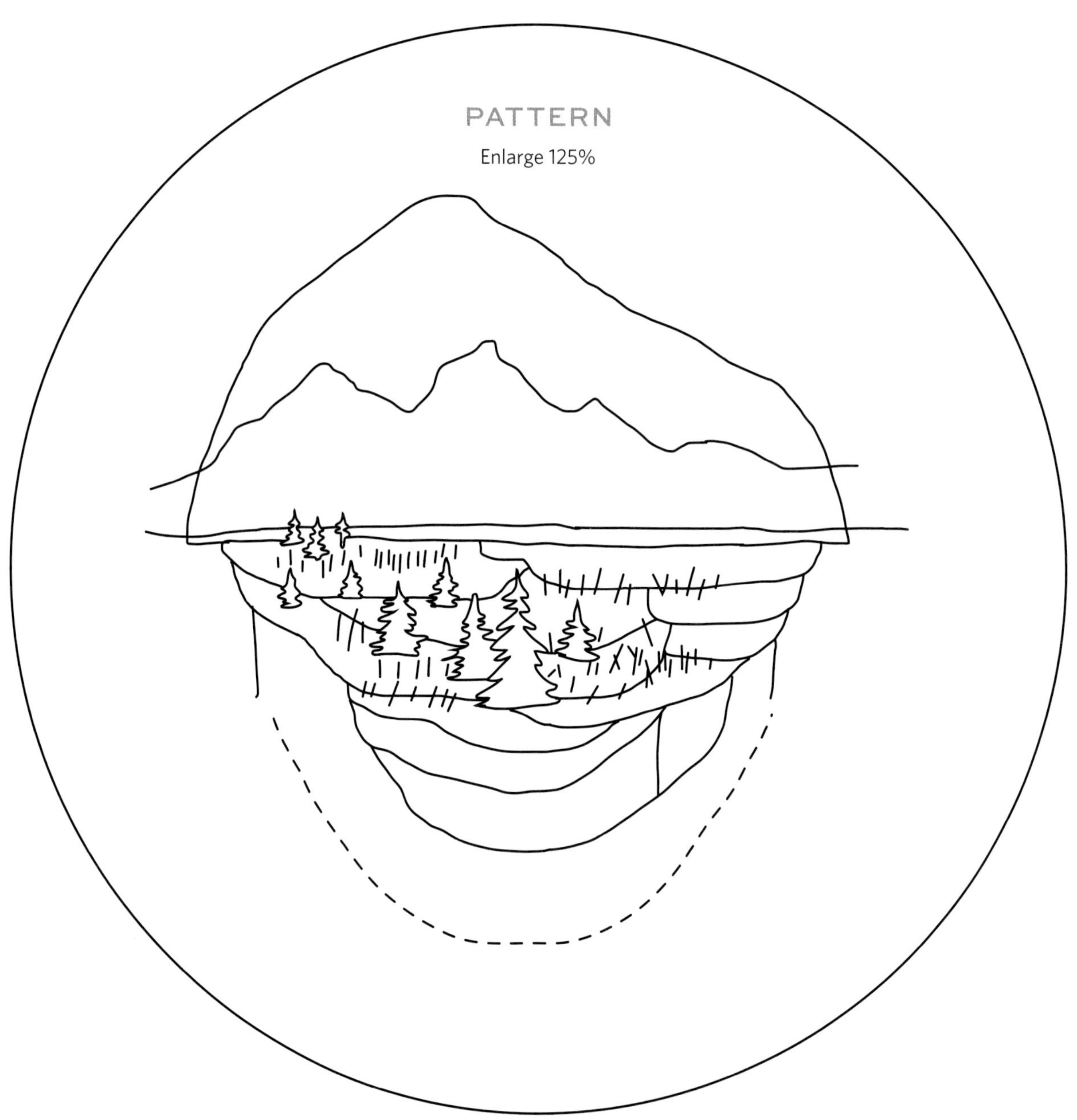
PATTERN
Enlarge 125%

## Transfer the Pattern

Using a water-soluble fabric marker, transfer the pattern onto the cloth.

## Stitch the Middle Ground

Use six-strand satin stitch in colors 833 and 937 to fill the top sections of the field closest to the horizon line.

In an area below the satin stitching, lay down the lima bean wool roving. Always use a little more than you think you need. Anchor the roving with four six-strand stitches in colors 833 and 937 that extend from the satin-stitched area into the top edge of the wool. Seal in the wool roving by filling the section below the wool with satin stitches made using two strands of pearl cotton in color 501. Catch the bottom of the wool as you finish each stitch.

Using colors 833, 3011, and 934, continue to fill in all the remaining sections with six-strand satin stitches.

## Stitch the Background

Use the pattern on page 169 to cut the sky from blue fabric. Attach it to the base fabric with double-sided tape.

Use a two-strand straight stitch in color 934 to create the horizon line. The stitches should be about 2" long and overlap each other to build a full-bodied line. Stitch on top of the sky fabric to help secure it. Suggest treetops in the distance with a few straight stitches in 934.

Use two-strand couched straight stitches in 934 to create the shape of the mountains.

## Stitch the Foreground

Use two-strand straight stitches to create grass on top of the satin-stitched middle ground in colors 833, 934, and 3011.

In colors 501, 833, 3011, and 934, add drips with 1"–2" two-strand straight stitches extending from the bottom of the satin stitch middle ground.

The Douglas fir trees here are a bit more detailed than the building block on page 132 because I'm featuring them in the foreground instead of the background. Create the trees with two-strand straight stitches in color 934. Create each trunk with a vertical straight stitch the height of the tree. Build the tree's shape with angled straight stitches. The smallest trees in the back should have about 4 stitches on each side of the trunk, while the larger ones in the foreground may have up to 20 per side.

## Finish the Hoop

Run your entire hoop under hot water to wash out the pattern transfer marks and tighten your fabric. Refer to Finishing Your Embroidery (page 56).

# MIDSUMMER'S GARDEN

In midsummer my garden becomes dark green with lush foliage. I wanted to capture that effect with watercolor placed above the horizon line to serve as a backdrop for brilliant floral color. In this garden you will find echinacea, calendula, bachelor's buttons, dandelion seed heads, and prairie coneflowers dancing amid five shades of summer green. I invite you to add or substitute flower varieties from your own garden or other favorites.

This pattern is one of the most ambitious because there are a lot of layers, and you'll have to improvise where you place the flowers instead of relying on the pattern outline. I recommend practicing the flowers on scrap fabric to get a feel for their curves and lines.

## BUILDING BLOCKS

Dry-Painted Sky, pages 120–121

Echinacea, pages 124–125

Calendula, pages 122–123

Bachelor's Buttons, pages 122–123

Prairie Coneflower, pages 128–129

Abstract Flowers, page 143

## COLOR AND STITCH GUIDE

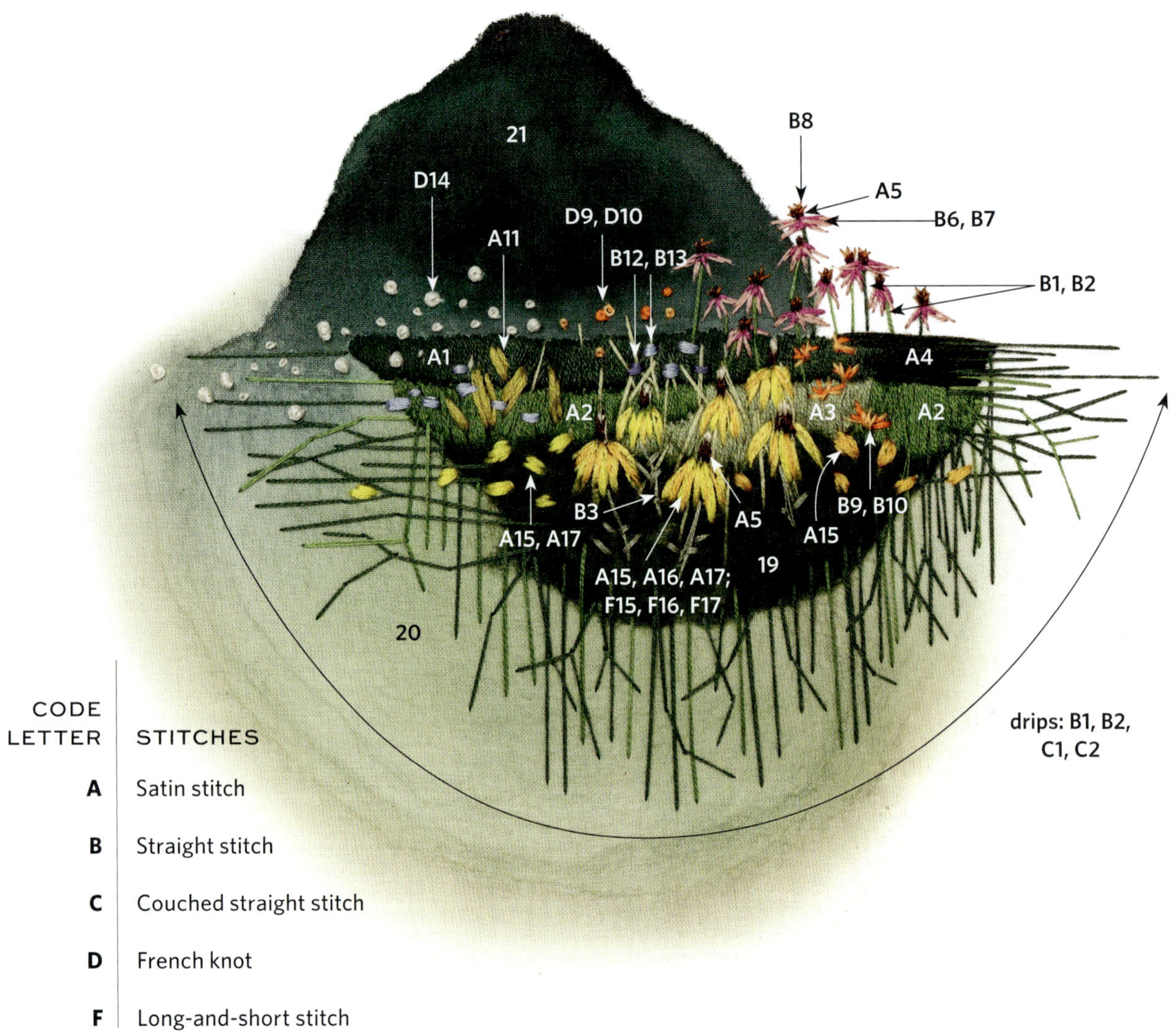


| CODE LETTER | STITCHES |
|---|---|
| **A** | Satin stitch |
| **B** | Straight stitch |
| **C** | Couched straight stitch |
| **D** | French knot |
| **F** | Long-and-short stitch |

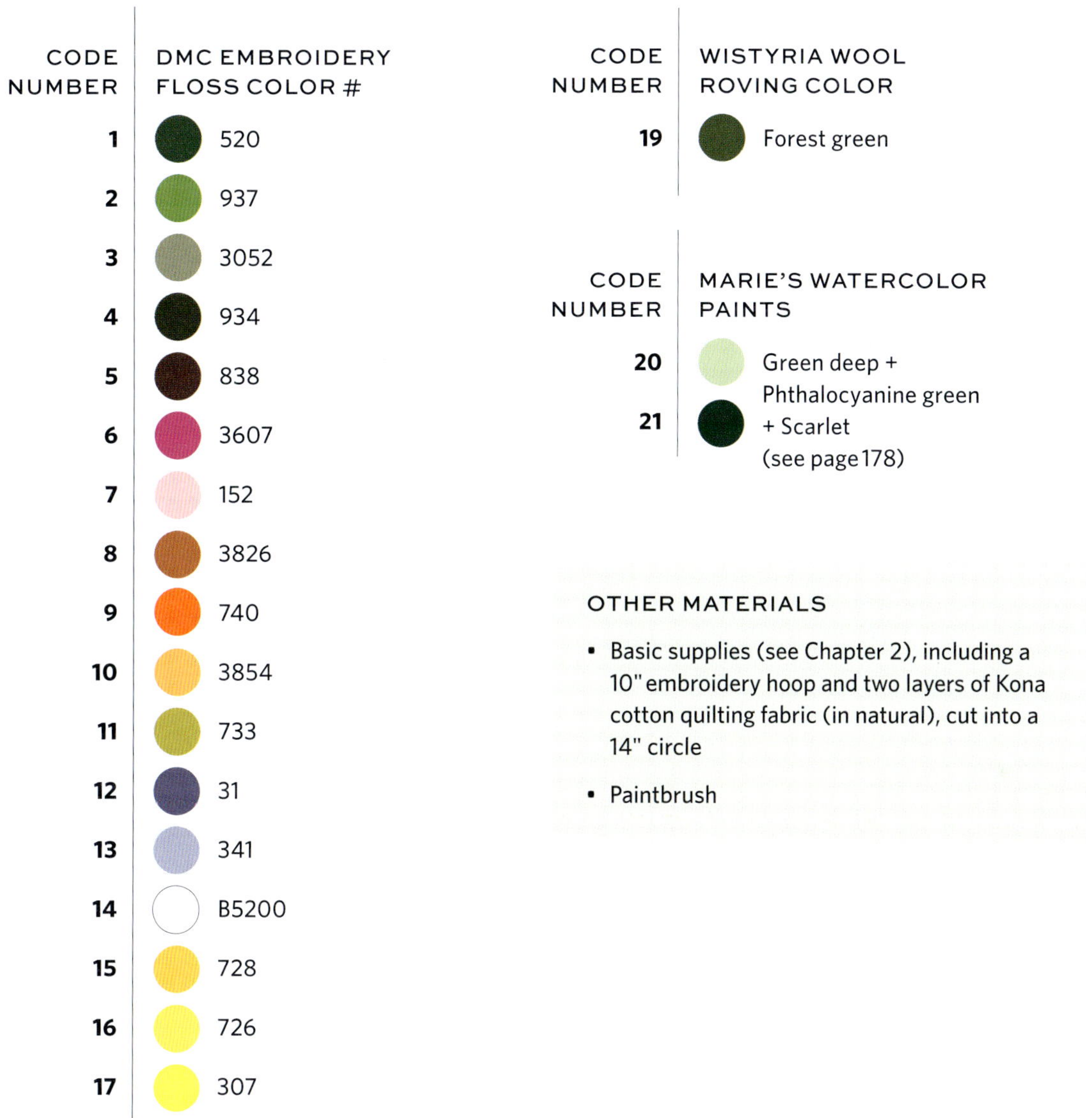

| CODE NUMBER | DMC EMBROIDERY FLOSS COLOR # |
|---|---|
| **1** | 520 |
| **2** | 937 |
| **3** | 3052 |
| **4** | 934 |
| **5** | 838 |
| **6** | 3607 |
| **7** | 152 |
| **8** | 3826 |
| **9** | 740 |
| **10** | 3854 |
| **11** | 733 |
| **12** | 31 |
| **13** | 341 |
| **14** | B5200 |
| **15** | 728 |
| **16** | 726 |
| **17** | 307 |

| CODE NUMBER | WISTYRIA WOOL ROVING COLOR |
|---|---|
| **19** | Forest green |

| CODE NUMBER | MARIE'S WATERCOLOR PAINTS |
|---|---|
| **20** | Green deep + Phthalocyanine green |
| **21** | + Scarlet (see page 178) |

### OTHER MATERIALS

- Basic supplies (see Chapter 2), including a 10" embroidery hoop and two layers of Kona cotton quilting fabric (in natural), cut into a 14" circle
- Paintbrush

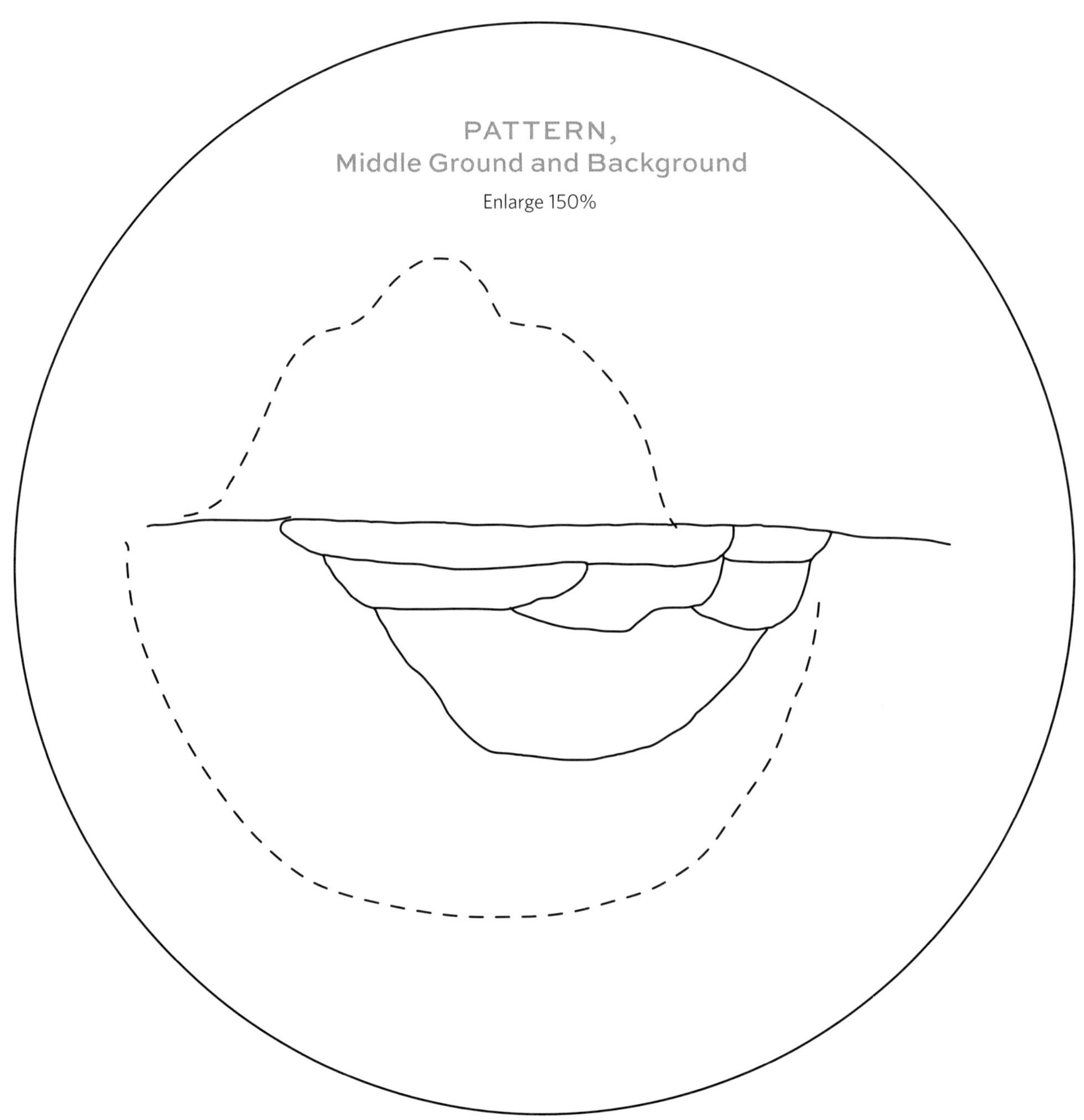
PATTERN,
Middle Ground and Background
Enlarge 150%

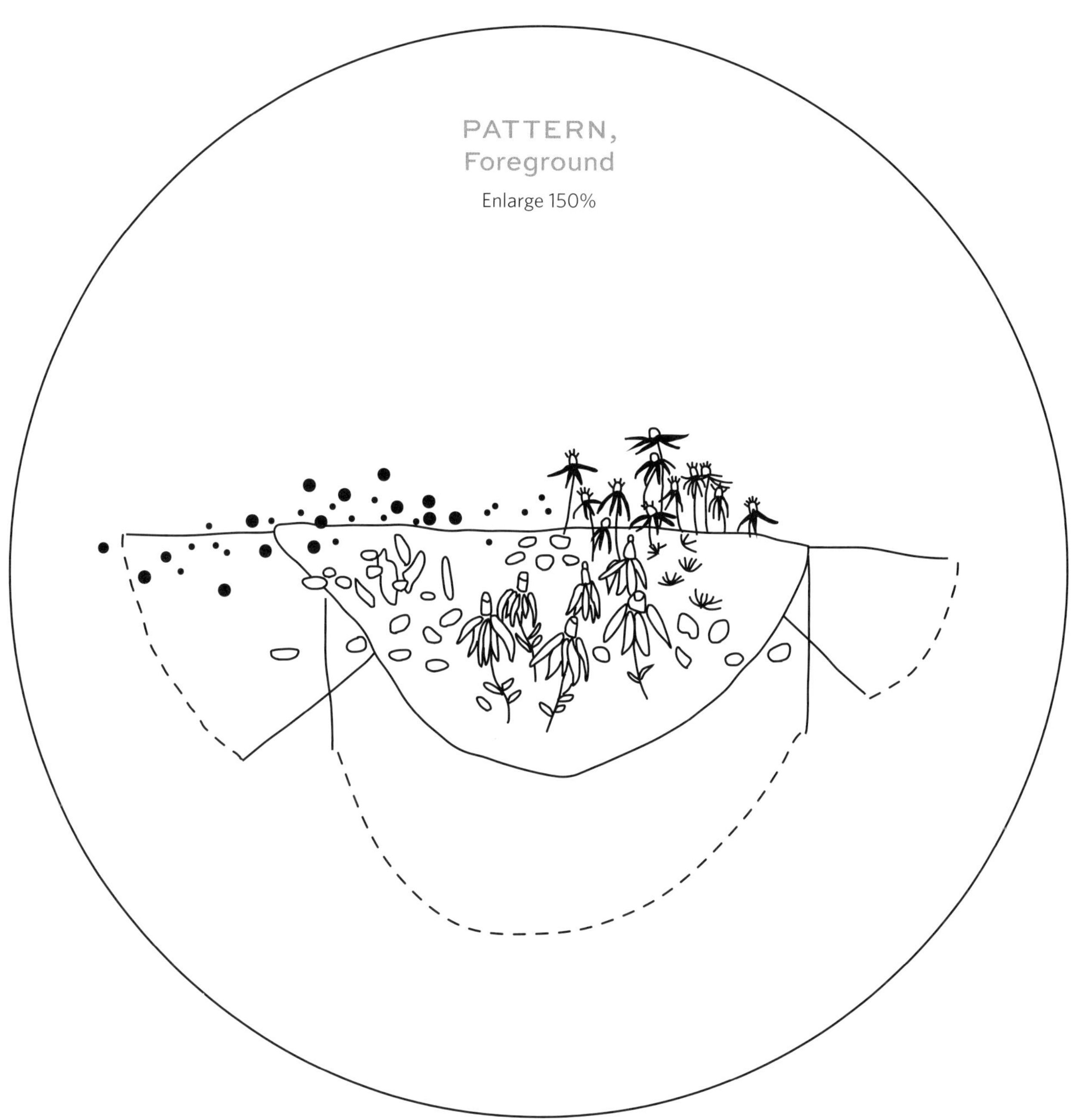
PATTERN,
Foreground
Enlarge 150%

## Transfer the Pattern

Using a water-soluble fabric marker, transfer the base pattern onto the cloth. There is no need to trace the foreground pattern.

## Stitch the Middle Ground

Use six-strand satin stitches to fill the top sections of the field closest to the horizon line in colors 520, 937, 3052, and 934.

## Run the Hoop Under Water

Run your entire hoop under hot water to wash out the pattern transfer marks and tighten your fabric. Let it dry before painting.

## Paint the Watercolor

There are two different greens in this piece. The green above the horizon line is cool, and the green below is warm. Make sure you practice on scrap fabric before you apply paint to your final piece!

For the warm green (number 20), mix three parts green deep with one part phthalocyanine green. Add a drop of scarlet to dull the color. A little goes a long way. Add a touch of water to the paint—enough to make it easy to spread but not watery.

For the cool green (number 21), mix one part green deep with three parts phthalocyanine green and a drop of scarlet. Add just enough water to the paint to make it easy to spread.

Apply clean water with a clean paintbrush around the bottom of the middle ground, soaking a circumference of about 3" around the satin stitches. Only get the bottom of the piece wet. Everything above the horizon line should remain dry. Dab little dots of warm green every ½" along the wet area, letting the paint bleed.

Without first wetting the area, apply cool green paint above the horizon line, creating the background shape.

Dry completely before moving on.

## Transfer the Next Pattern

Using a heat-erasable pen, trace or draw the drip area. You won't be able to transfer the foreground details, but you can use the pattern or the stitch guide to eyeball placement of those stitches.

## Finish the Middle Ground

In an area below the satin stitching, lay down some wool roving. Always use a little more than you think you need. Anchor the roving with 10 stitches using six strands of 937 and 3052 that extend from the satin-stitched areas into the top edge of the wool. Seal in the wool roving with two-strand straight stitches and couched straight stitches that create drips in colors 520 and 937. Catch the bottom edge of the wool as you finish each stitch.

Along the sides of the drip area, add horizontal two-strand straight stitches and couched straight stitches 1"–2" long in colors 520 and 937.

## Stitch the Foreground

It's time to add the flowers! You can stitch them in any order, but I typically start from the top and work my way down.

**ECHINACEA:** Use two-strand satin stitch in color 838 for the flower center. Each petal is made using a two-strand straight stitch by combining one longer stitch and one shorter stitch in different colors. Beginning with color 3607, create stitches that are half the length of the petal and attach to the flower head. Then stitch the points of the petals with color 152, bringing the needle up at the tip of the petal and blending with thread 3607. Add several single-strand straight stitches to the flower head in color 3826 to create echinacea's trademark spikes. For efficiency, wait to add the stems until you've completed the other flower varieties.

**CALENDULA:** Use two-strand straight stitches to create the petals in colors 740 and 3854. Each petal should meet at a central point. For calendula blossoms along the horizon line, use two-strand floss to stitch a few French knots wrapped two times around the needle.

**LETTUCE:** For a gestural suggestion of lettuce heads, use six-strand satin stitch in color 733.

**BACHELOR'S BUTTONS:** Use horizontal six-strand straight stitches about ¼" long in colors 31 and 341 to create rounded flower heads. These stitches can easily pull the threads below apart, so take care to leave the stitches slightly loose.

**DANDELIONS:** In color B5200, French knot the seed heads with two-strand floss wrapped one to three times around the needle to create a variety of sizes.

**PRAIRIE CONEFLOWER:** As with the echinacea, use two-strand satin stitch for the flower heads in color 838. Using a combination of colors 728, 726, and 307 for each flower, create each petal with two six-strand satin stitches on top of each other. Begin with the darkest yellow and make three or four petals. Switch to the midtone yellow and make two or three petals. Finish with the highlight yellow for another two or three petals. Use a long-and-short stitch of varying shades to add detailed value to a few petals on each flower.

**FLOWER STEMS:** In color 3052 for calendula and prairie coneflower and colors 937 and 520 for echinacea, use two-strand straight stitches to add stems to the flowers. Use shorter two-strand straight stitches to create leaves on the prairie coneflower.

**ABSTRACT FLOWERS:** Use six-strand satin stitches in colors 307 and 728 to create the rest of the yellow flowers dotting the landscape.

## Finish the Hoop

Use a hair dryer to remove any residual markings. Refer to Finishing Your Embroidery (page 56).

# GARDEN BOUNTY

Toward the end of summer, the garden overflows with flowers and vegetables. I wanted to create a hoop that captured this abundance. This project is perfect to pick up in winter when you're longing for your garden. Note that I chose lighter greens for the beets and carrots than what I specified in the building blocks, because I needed a color that would stand out against the base of watercolor. Building blocks are always just starting points!

## BUILDING BLOCKS

Salvia, pages 128–129

Oriental Poppies, pages 126–127

Yarrow, page 130

Pumpkins, pages 138–139

Carrots, pages 138–139

Beets, pages 138–139

Abstract Flowers (white dandelions), page 143

## COLOR AND STITCH GUIDE

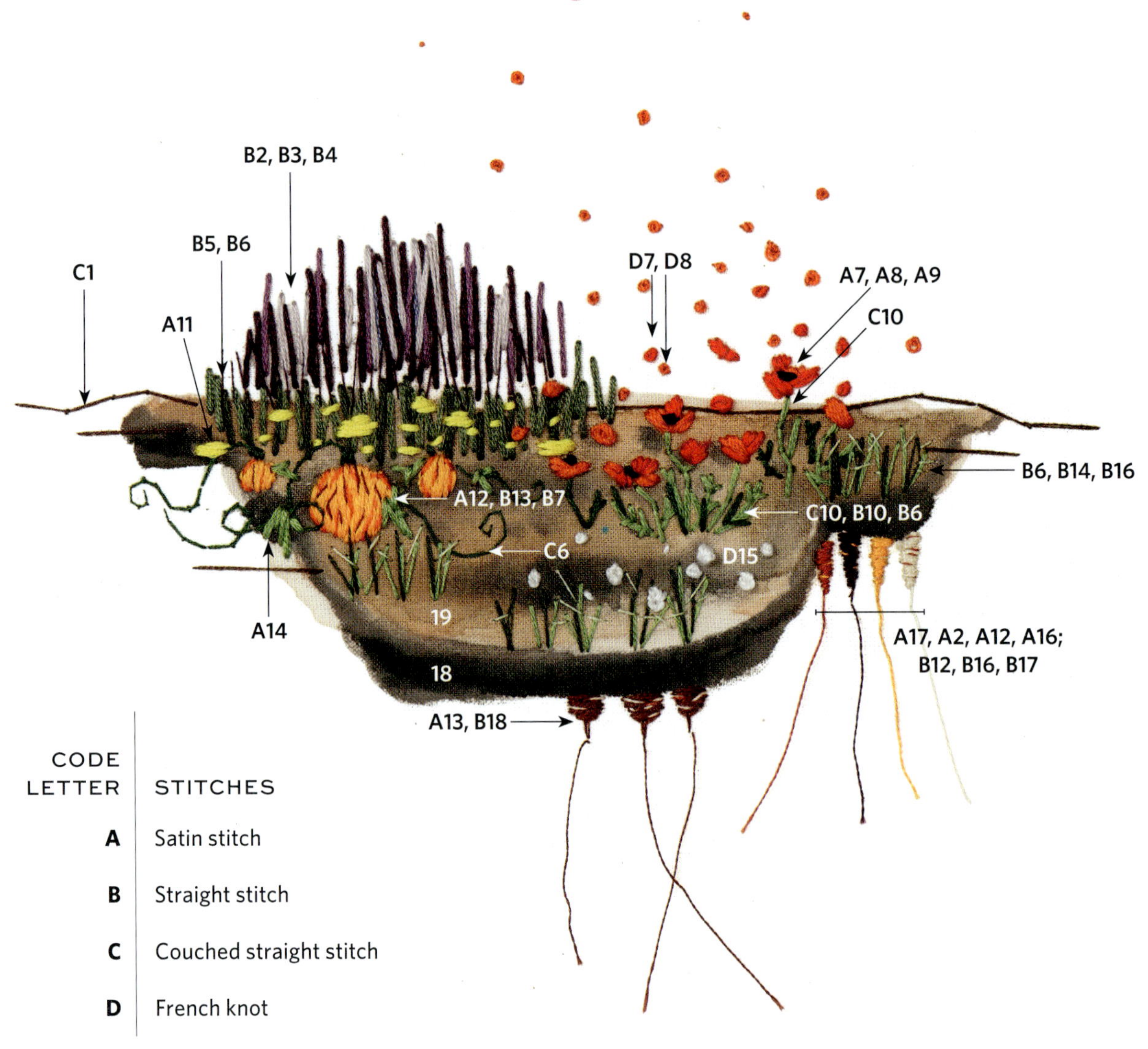


| CODE LETTER | STITCHES |
|---|---|
| **A** | Satin stitch |
| **B** | Straight stitch |
| **C** | Couched straight stitch |
| **D** | French knot |

| CODE NUMBER | DMC EMBROIDERY FLOSS COLOR # |
|---|---|
| **1** | 3781 |
| **2** | 154 |
| **3** | 327 |
| **4** | 3042 |
| **5** | 3362 |
| **6** | 935 |
| **7** | 900 |
| **8** | 666 |
| **9** | 310 |
| **10** | 987 |
| **11** | 307 |
| **12** | 741 |
| **13** | 3857 |
| **14** | 988 |
| **15** | B5200 |
| **16** | 739 |
| **17** | 22 |
| **18** | 819 |

| CODE NUMBER | MARIE'S WATERCOLOR PAINTS |
|---|---|
| **18** | Green deep + Scarlet |
| **19** | Green deep + Scarlet + Burnt sienna |

### OTHER MATERIALS

- Basic supplies (see Chapter 2), including a 10" embroidery hoop and two layers of Kona cotton quilting fabric (in natural), cut into a 14" circle
- Paintbrush

## PATTERN

Enlarge 150%

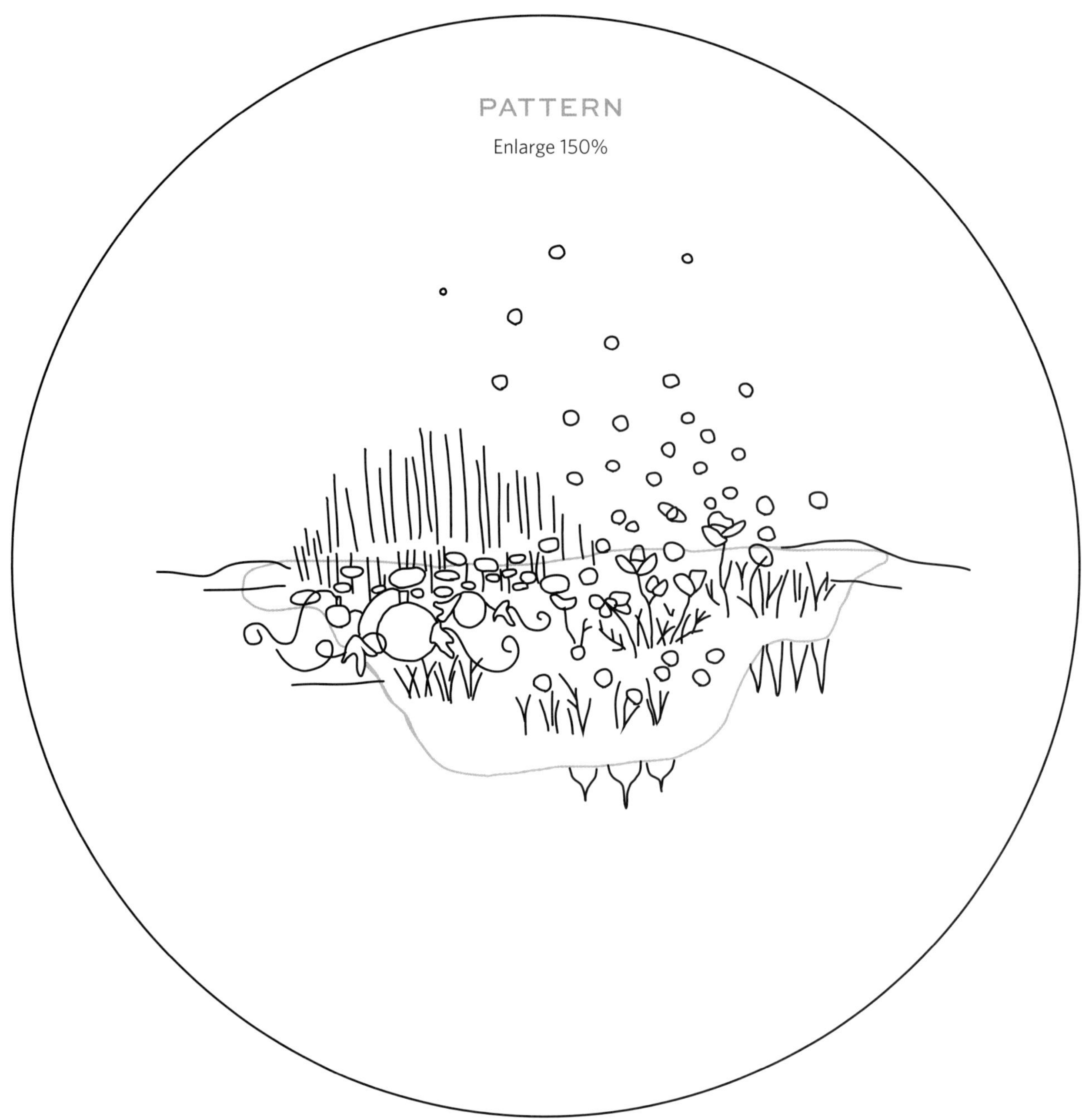

## Prepare the Hoop

Run the hoop and fabric under hot water to tighten and smooth your fabric.

## Transfer the Pattern

Using a heat-erasable pen, transfer the pattern onto the cloth.

## Paint the Watercolor

To create the dark brown color for the bottom of the watercolor area, mix equal parts green deep and scarlet. You may need to add a bit of extra green to get a true brown.

To create a lighter brown for the top of the watercolor area, separate a portion of the dark brown and mix in an equal amount of burnt sienna. Add water to the paint until the consistency is thin, both to lighten the color further and to ensure the cloth remains supple enough to stitch through.

Apply the watery, light brown paint to the top of the dirt patch.

Dry the brush. Fill the lower border of the dirt patch with dark brown paint. Take a few dabs of the dark brown to dot and streak the light brown area.

Let dry completely before moving on.

## Stitch the Background

Use a two-strand couched straight stitch in color 3781 for the horizon line, leaving a break where you will stitch the salvia.

## Stitch the Foreground

It's time to add the flowers!

**SALVIA:** Use a six-strand straight stitch about 1" long for each flower. Vary the shades of purple throughout the flower patch using colors 154, 327, and 3042. Also use six-strand straight stitches in colors 3362 and 935 for the stems and a single-strand straight stitch in color 154 to connect the flower to the stems.

**ORIENTAL POPPIES:** Create the petals with a combination of six-strand satin stitches in colors 900 and 666. Add the black center with four-strand satin stitch in color 310. Use four-strand couched straight stitches for the stems in color 987. For the center of each leaf, use a four-strand straight stitch. Add lobes to the leaves with shorter four-strand straight stitches in colors 987 and 935. In colors 900 and 666, finish the field of poppies by adding French knots of varied sizes in the distance, stitched with two-strand floss wrapped around the needle one to four times.

**YARROW:** Use six-strand satin stitches in color 307.

**PUMPKINS:** Use six-strand satin stitches in color 741 for the body of each pumpkin with two-strand straight stitches in color 3857 layered on top and single-strand straight stitches in color 900 for the ridges. Use two-strand couched straight stitches in color 935 for the vines with a few single-strand couched straight stitches for the tendrils. Add leaves with six-strand satin stitch in color 988.

**DANDELIONS:** In color B5200, French knot simple dandelion seed heads in varied sizes, with two-strand floss wrapped one to four times around the needle.

**CARROT AND BEET TOPS:** Use two-strand straight stitches in colors 935 and 988 for the tops of the beets and carrots. Add a few leaves to the tops with single-strand straight stitches in color 739.

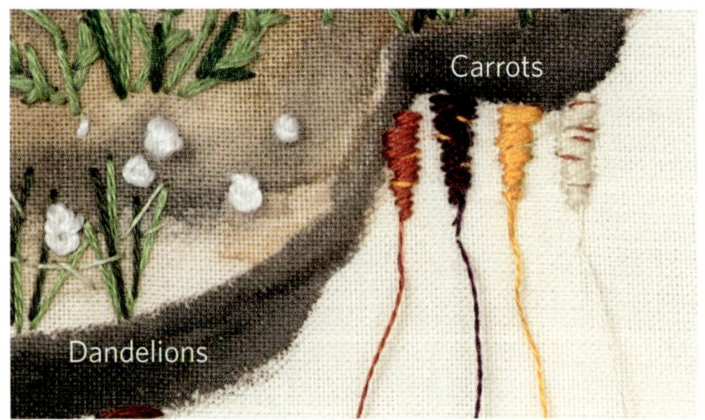

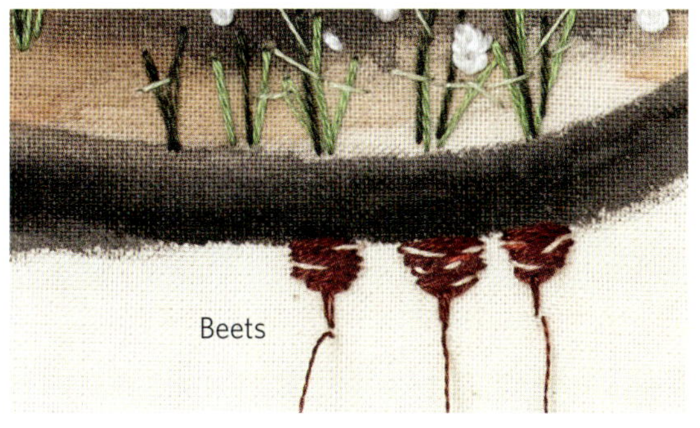


**CARROT AND BEET ROOTS:** Use four-strand satin stitches in color 3857 for the beets and colors 22, 154, 741, and 739 for the carrots. Add texture to the roots with single-strand straight stitches in color 819 for the beet, 741 for the red carrot, 739 for the purple and orange carrots, and 22 for the white carrot. Extend the roots of the beets and carrots by threading the needle with a single strand of floss, well knotted at one end. Pull the needle through at the base of the root, then cut the thread so it hangs freely.

## Finish the Hoop

Use a hair dryer to remove any residual markings. Refer to Finishing Your Embroidery (page 56).

CHAPTER 8

# COMPOSING ORIGINAL LANDSCAPES

Congratulations! If you've practiced stitching landscapes using the patterns in Chapters 5 and 7, you have the skills to make an original work of art based on a corner of the earth that you love. I know you can do it. Let's get going!

# DESIGNING THE LANDSCAPE

You'll start by developing a sketch based on your own observations of a landscape, and then you'll turn that into a basic pattern. Refer to Chapters 5, 6, and 7 for ideas on how to fill in your middle ground, background, and foreground. Remember that if you can't find a plant you want in the building blocks, you can always create your own (see Creating Your Own Building Block, page 134).

## Build the Sketch

When sketching the composition of a landscape embroidery, I tend to work in sequential steps. Because I always leave negative space around the edges, the finished shape of my landscape usually looks sort of like a large blob.

**1.** To begin, you need to observe and sketch the landscape that will inspire the piece. (See Chapter 1, Connecting to the Land.) Gather those sketches and any photos that will support your work.

**2.** Trace a 5" or 6" embroidery hoop to create a circle template for sketching the composition.

**3.** Sketch the horizon line and add the general shape of the land under it.

**4.** Add a sky shape if you plan on having one.

**5.** Add details to the land to create movement. (See Map the Movement, page 15.)

**6.** Sketch details like trees or flowers on the horizon line.

**7.** Once you've drawn a pencil sketch, add basic color. I like to use colored pencils or watercolor for this step. You aren't looking to show every color of thread; simply indicate the colors of different sections.

## Transfer the Sketch

Prepare the hoop and draw the composition on your fabric with a water-soluble fabric marker. If you don't feel confident drawing freehand,

### The Horizon Line

This simple line is the anchor of your composition, creating the ground for the entire piece. When you are sketching, always start with the horizon line. When you stitch, make sure the horizon line is clearly and boldly marked so that you can position everything else in relation to it.

## Cheat Sheet for Making a Landscape Look Natural

Variation and observation are the key elements that make an embroidered landscape look natural.

- Make irregular, organic lines. The couched straight stitch is your friend.
- Create inconsistency in direction, placement, and size of stitches.
- Ensure you have a full range of values, from the darkest dark to the lightest lights.
- Look at your source of inspiration closely as you work.

redraw the sketch on paper at the finished size you want or enlarge it using a scanner. Now trace the drawing with a black marker and transfer it onto the fabric. (See Transferring Your Design, page 38.)

## Choose Thread Colors

Think of choosing your threads as if you were a painter preparing a color palette. You want a large selection of colors available as you're working, even if you don't use all of them. I like to go to my local craft store and stand in their embroidery floss section with a photo of my landscape in hand. Hold threads up to the photo to see if they are a good match.

Make sure you select a variety of very dark, midtone, and very light versions of the colors you are using for the middle ground. When choosing colors for the foreground, you'll want colors that contrast significantly with the middle ground. I am often surprised at how a color that seems way too bright will in fact be exactly what I need for my foreground. Review Choosing Your Colors on pages 34–37 for more guidance on understanding color and selecting threads.

## Begin the Stitching

Always begin the landscape by building the middle ground with satin stitching or sections of wool roving. The middle ground is the base onto which you'll layer details for depth. I recommend starting at the top nearest the horizon line and working down from there. To create a sense of perspective, the stitches at the top should be the smallest and get gradually larger as they move toward the bottom of the hoop.

## Sketch Again

When you're done stitching the middle ground, I recommend revisiting and refining your composition. To do this, snap a picture with your phone of what you've embroidered. Most phones have a paint tool you can use to draw on top of a photo. Mine is found in the edit function of my phone's default photo app. Use this painting tool to draw out the foreground and background of your embroidery. You can also print the image and physically draw on it if you prefer. As with your original sketch, keep these marks very basic to further test composition and color choices.

## Finish the Stitching

Once you are happy with the middle ground and you've made a second pass at sketching the remaining elements of the composition, stitch the background. It might be as simple as a horizon line and a few trees in the distance, or it could be more complex, like a collaged fabric sky.

Now you are ready for the most fun and exciting part! Remember that foreground details should add movement to the composition. They can also connect disparate parts of the middle ground. When combining wool roving and satin stitching, for example, foreground details placed across both elements can make them more cohesive.

Refine a work in progress by taking a photo and using a painting app to sketch again.

## Argh! I Hate It!

I'm often working on a piece and get to a point where I think, "This just isn't working." Here's a secret: This is an exciting and pivotal moment in your work. Every one of my most successful pieces has had a moment like this. My least successful pieces usually don't.

This is an opportunity to reconsider everything you originally thought was going to work. You look for other options, and usually the expansion of your thinking brings the work to the next level. Embrace the difficulty of the moment, and don't be discouraged if it happens more than once in a single embroidery project!

To diagnose what isn't working, I have two suggestions. First, take a photo of the piece and use the process described in Sketch Again (on the opposite page) to try out new ideas. Sketching is much faster than stitching and will help you see where you might need to add a few details or even expand the middle ground or background.

Second, I suggest hanging the unfinished piece on your wall and living with it for a while. Seeing the composition out of the corner of your eye and from a distance—without the pressure of actively trying to solve the problem—sometimes brings an "aha" moment about what you need to change or add.

# FINDING YOUR STYLE

I've shared how I envision landscape embroidery and how to design and stitch landscapes in my style, but here's something you might not know. You have your own style. It just needs to be discovered . . . by you!

When I first started embroidering, I didn't set out with the goal of creating abstract landscapes. I was just interested in making thread paintings of trees, birds, and plants. Over time I started stitching scenes. First I tried a field of grass. Later I added watercolor. Next, fabric collage. I developed a vision for what I wanted: enough realism that viewers would immediately recognize the subject of the image but enough abstraction that I had space to intentionally design line quality, composition, and color. I spent three years on new ideas before I had a piece that expressed that vision.

Now that I look back at my early work, I see not only an evolution but also a continuity—something ineffable and subtle that makes all my pieces uniquely mine. Something people call my style. With consistent practice and time, your style will develop. You'll start seeing little things that make your work uniquely yours. Here are some tips to help you along the way.

## Start with What You Know

When I was in art school, I had this idea that to become a great artist I needed to master a historically celebrated medium like sculpting marble, fabricating wooden installations, or painting with oils. What I was always drawn to, though, was simple graphite on paper. My ability to master complicated mediums felt lacking. Having children brought even more limitations on the kind of materials I could use, but I discovered along the way that whenever I leaned into a familiar medium I enjoyed, my own personal style started to come to life in my work. I embroidered for five years before experimenting with techniques like watercolor, wool roving, and collage. I laid a foundation of skill where my own style could blossom in time.

## Get Playful

If you enjoy embroidery, practice. If there is another medium you enjoy, practice. Once you feel established in one or more mediums you know and love, start playing! Imagine yourself as a child who's just been handed a needle and thread. What is that child going to do with it? What limits will you push? Can you stitch on wood? How do you get a piece of fabric to stand straight up without falling over? Can you make an embroidery the size of a wall? As adults we

often roll our eyes at fanciful ideas, but I encourage you to release your inner child whenever you step into your creative space and imagine the impossible—because it just might be more possible than you thought.

## Use Inspiration Intentionally

When you find an artist or a scene from nature that inspires you, think about what draws you to it. Is it the composition? The content? Or do you love the color palette? Then think about how you can weave those elements into your own work. While making direct copies of other artists' work can help you learn certain processes and techniques, that isn't the best route for developing your personal artistic style. When you discover with specificity what you love in nature or in other artists' work, you create a fusion of ideas and inspiration that become the origin of your own personal style.

## Keep a Sketchbook

Our world is saturated with digital ways to bookmark inspiration, but I encourage documenting what you love in a sketchbook. Your sources of inspiration become more tangible, and they infuse your work more readily. You can print out photos that inspire you and glue them in, sketch vignettes or scenes in nature that catch your eye, create compositional sketches of works of art you love, and tape dried flowers and grasses right onto your paper. Any way that you can use your *hands* instead of looking at a screen will benefit your art practice.

## Keep a Record

When I'm in an artistic rut, the first thing I do is gather my old sketchbooks and start flipping through them. Doing this every few months makes it easy to see the thread that connects my work together. Recently I picked up an old sketchbook and, to my surprise, found a lot of writing from years ago about how I wanted to find a way to explore and express the subtle and ordinary in my work. That pursuit still has resonance for me and is exactly what I was trying to express in a study of dead grass that I was working on. Looking back at old ideas helps you home in on what exactly your art is about.

Above all, be patient and enjoy the process!

# BUILDING-BLOCK PATTERNS

Following are transfer patterns for the designs in Chapter 6. You will need to adjust their scale to work for your specific embroidery.

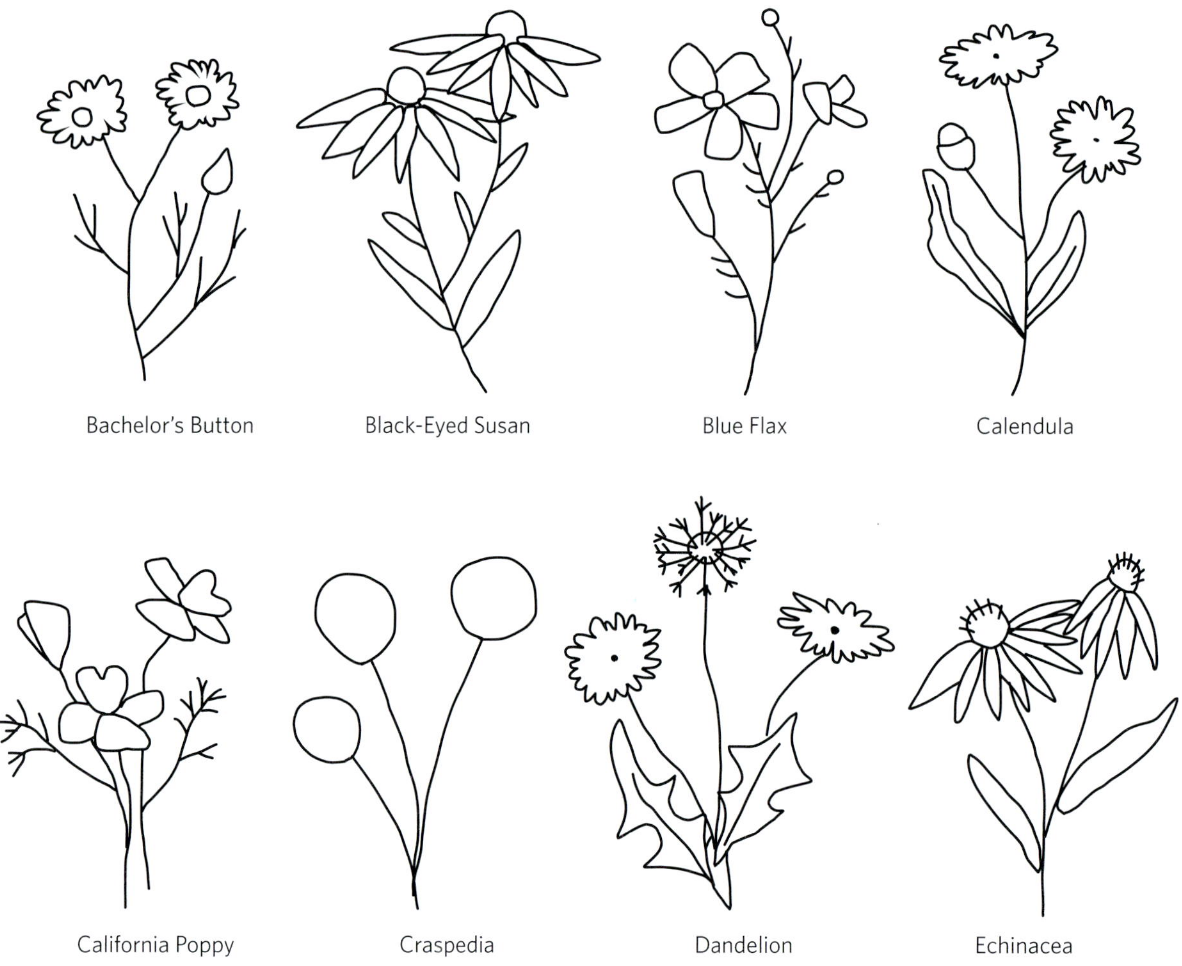

Bachelor's Button | Black-Eyed Susan | Blue Flax | Calendula

California Poppy | Craspedia | Dandelion | Echinacea

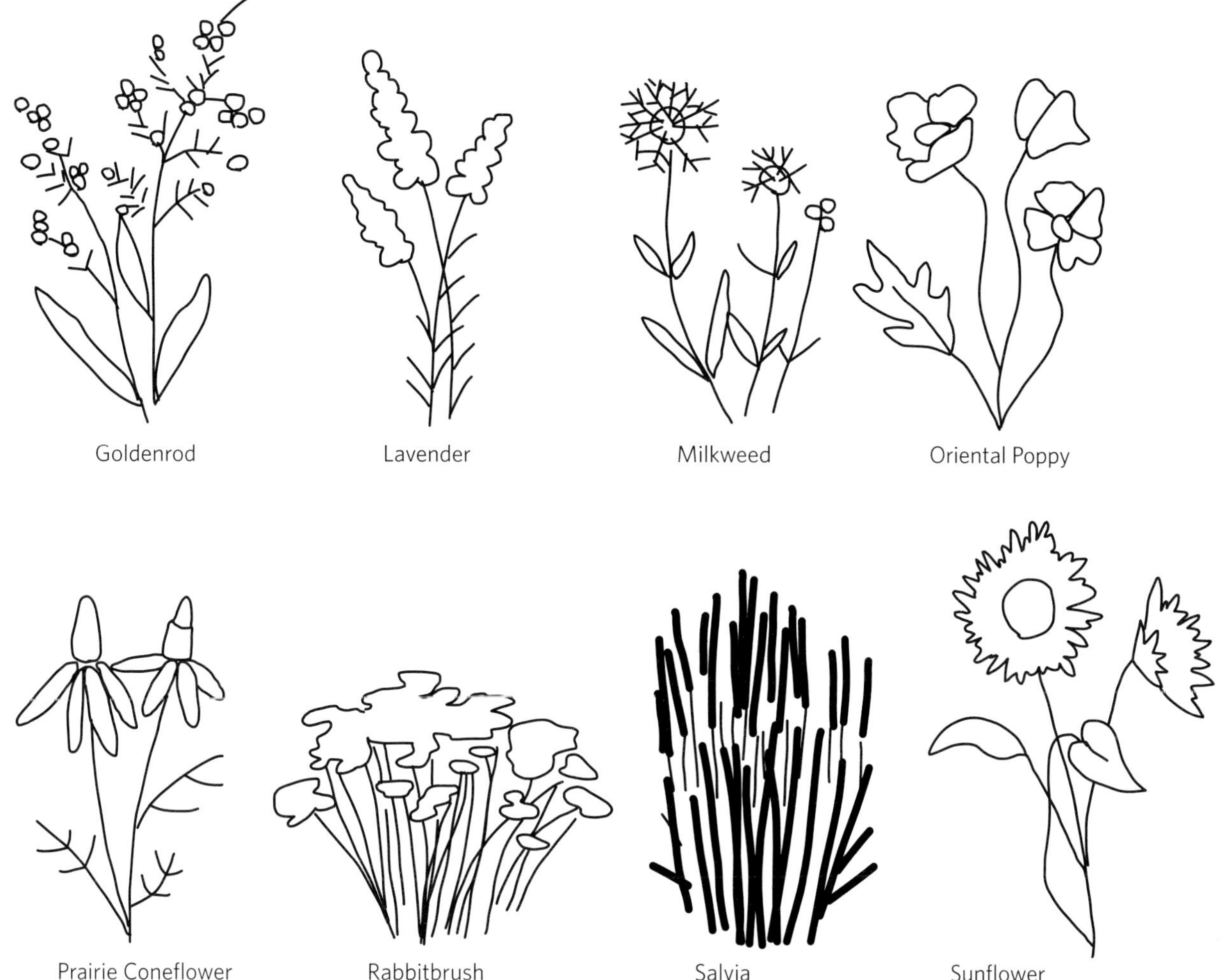
Goldenrod
Lavender
Milkweed
Oriental Poppy
Prairie Coneflower
Rabbitbrush
Salvia
Sunflower

Thistle
Yarrow
Tree Shapes
Blue Spruce
Douglas Fir
Maple
Oak
Rocky Mountain Juniper
Big Bluestem
Blue Fescue
Blue Grama
Switchgrass

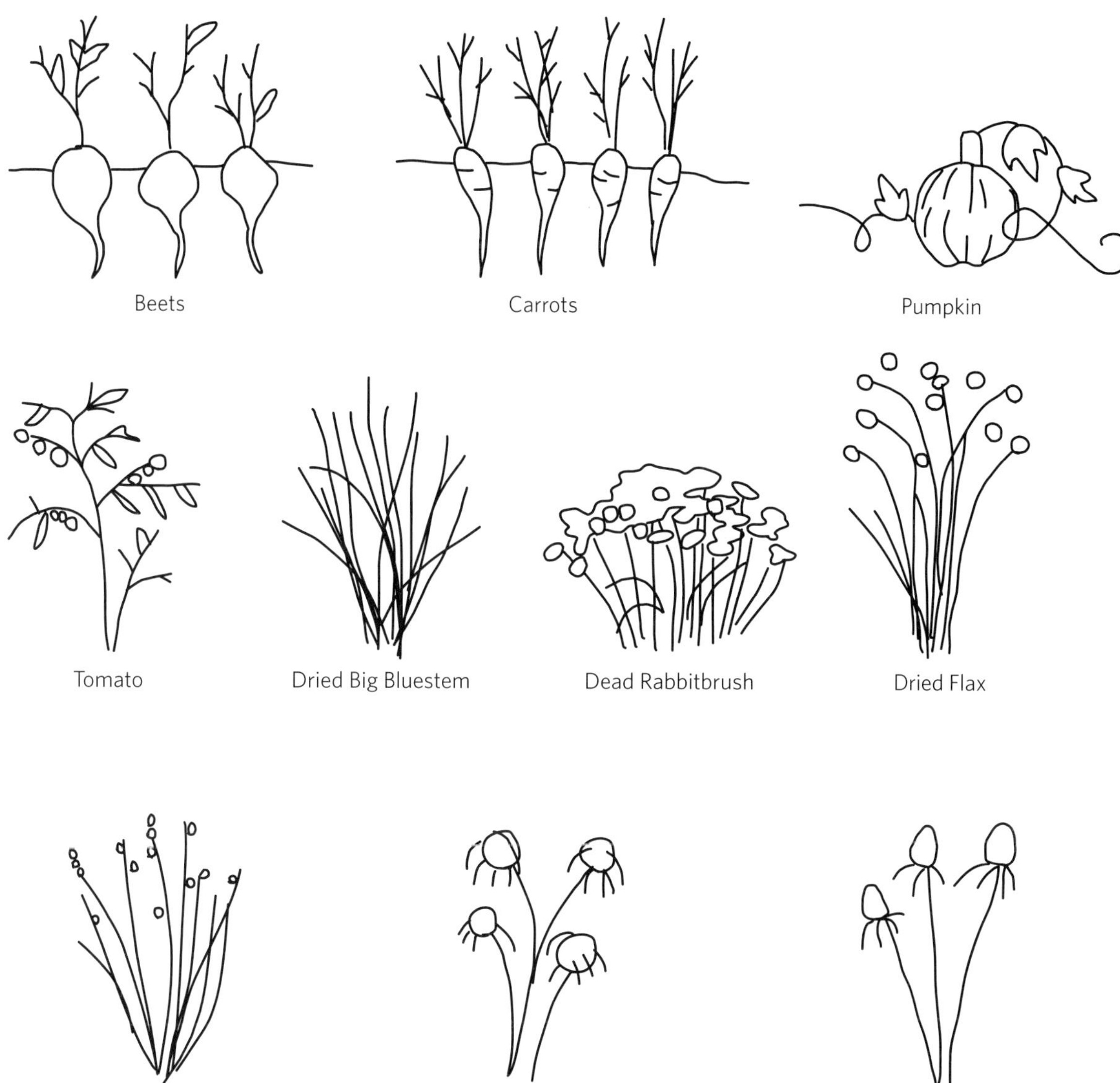
Beets
Carrots
Pumpkin
Tomato
Dried Big Bluestem
Dead Rabbitbrush
Dried Flax
Dried Switchgrass
Sunflower Seed Heads
Echinacea Seed Heads

# RESOURCES

## Materials

Caydo embroidery hoops: https://caydo.com

DMC floss, thread, and wool: https://dmc.com/US/en, (800) 275-4117

Kona cotton quilting fabric: https://robertkaufman.com/fabrics/kona_cotton/, (800) 877-2066

Marie's Water Colour paints: available at art supply stores

The ThreadGatherer: https://threadgatherer.com

US Art Supply (supply boxes): https://usartsupply.com/, (858) 909-2110

Wistyria wool roving: https://wistyria.com

## Art Inspiration and Art Career

Aoki, Kazuko. *Embroidered Garden Flowers: Botanical Motifs for Needle and Thread*. Roost Books, 2017.

Bayles, David, and Ted Orland. *Art & Fear: Observations on the Perils (and Rewards) of Artmaking*. Imagine Continuum Press, 2001.

Berger, John. *Ways of Seeing*. Penguin Books, 1990.

Bhandari, Heather Darcy, and Jonathan Melber. *Art/Work: Everything You Need to Know (and Do) As You Pursue Your Art Career*. Free Press, 2009.

Botelho, Emily. *Abstract Embroidery: Slow Stitching with Texture, Colour and Creativity*. Search Press, 2024.

Corn, Wanda M. *The Art of Andrew Wyeth*. Fine Arts Museums of San Francisco, 1973.

Holton, Lauren. *The Modern Embroidery Studio: 20 Stylish Designs to Stitch, Wear, and Share*. Krause Craft, 2020.

Phaidon Editors. *Vitamin D3: Today's Best in Contemporary Drawing*. Phaidon Press, 2022.

Vannier, Charlotte. *From Thread to Needle: Contemporary Embroidery Art*. Gingko Press, 2019.

## Nature Inspiration

Berry, Wendell. *The Peace of Wild Things: And Other Poems*. Penguin Books, 2018.

———. *The Selected Poems of Wendell Berry*. Counterpoint, 1999.

Oliver, Mary. *A Thousand Mornings: Poems*. Penguin Books, 2013.

Wohlleben, Peter. *The Hidden Life of Trees: What They Feel, How They Communicate—Discoveries from a Secret World*. Greystone Books, 2016.

———. *The Secret Network of Nature: Trees, Animals, and the Extraordinary Balance of All Living Things—Stories from Science and Observation*. Greystone Books, 2019.

## Nature Reference

Brockman, C. Frank. *Trees of North America: A Guide to Field Identification.* Golden Guides from St. Martin's Press, 2001.

Venning, Frank D. *Wildflowers of North America: A Guide to Field Identification*. St. Martin's Press, 1984.

## Additional Embroidery Resources

DMC's step-by-step embroidery stitch guide: https://dmc.com/US/en/sbs-embroidery-stitch-diagrams

Ganderton, Lucinda. *Embroidery: The Ideal Guide to Stitching, Whatever Your Level of Expertise*. DK, 2022.


# ACKNOWLEDGMENTS


Lander, you are the butter to my bread, the breath to my life, the Paul to my Julia. Thank you for believing in me more than I ever believed in myself. August, Peter, and Beatrice: You bring life to my life and are the inspiration behind all that I do.

Thank you to my mom, who taught me to look closely at this good green earth.

Thank you to Memé, who gave me my first painting lesson and showed me how to find the darkest darks and lightest lights.

Thank you to my sisters. Debbie, for being the reason I knew I always wanted to be a mom, and for giving me such a beautiful picture of motherhood to grow into. And to Betsy for reading all the words in this book and then rereading them and reading them all again—for knowing my story so well that you knew exactly what I was trying to say even before I knew myself.

And Tim, thank you for reminding me to put the bottom line up front.

Last, but not least, thank you to Brooke for bringing light to my vision for this book.

# INDEX

Page numbers in *italics* indicate photos or illustrations; numbers in **bold** indicate charts.

## F



## G



## H



## L

## T



## U

## W